P9-DID-054

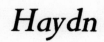

Haydn

THE GREAT COMPOSERS

HAYDN

by

H. C. ROBBINS LANDON

in association with

HENRY RAYNOR

PRAEGER PUBLISHERS

New York . Washington

BOOKS THAT MATTER
Published in the United States of America in 1972 by
Praeger Publishers, Inc., 111 Fourth Avenue,
New York, N.Y. 10003

Library of Congress Catalog Card Number: 70–185336

Printed in Great Britain

Contents

Illustrations

Music Examples

I

Childhood

Ever since the beginning of the nineteenth century, when he was an old man loaded with honours from every European country, Joseph Haydn has been accepted as one of the greatest composers. Before his life was over, while he was still writing the music of his splendid old age, Haydn was idolized as a supreme genius by men who realized even then that he is the father of modern instrumental music. He was the first composer to work out the possibilities of the symphony and the sonata and to show what their special qualities are. He was among the first musicians to establish the orchestra as we know it now. He was born in 1732 and lived to be seventy-seven; his life stretched from the age of Bach and Handel to that of Beethoven, and when he died, a twelve-year-old Franz Schubert had already started to compose. During his lifetime, music changed immeasurably, and many of the changes are the direct result of his work.

Although Haydn has always been accepted as a great composer, for many years the greater part of his work was neglected, and even today he is best known for the symphonies he wrote to be played in London between 1791 and 1795, when he was already an elderly man, and his 'London Symphonies' are only twelve out of more than a hundred and four works. His two German oratorios, *The Creation* and *The Seasons* share the fame of the London Symphonies, and so do a handful of his eighty-two string quartets. His operas were never performed, and his church music was rarely heard outside Austria and Germany, in the years between his death and the end of the Second World War. His piano sonatas, too, were almost forgotten, as were dozens of works in almost every musical form. It was not that he wrote a few great masterpieces and a great number of less important works, but simply that very little of his vast output of compositions remained fashionable.

We are living at a time when better justice is being done. Scholars are providing accurate new editions of his music and performers are discovering the attractiveness of many of his works which have been forgotten for a

13

century or more. Audiences have discovered a new interest in works for small orchestras as well as in music for the huge nineteenth-century symphony orchestra, and these new interests are enabling Haydn's music to come into its own. To understand all Haydn's music is not only to come to love its vigour, inventiveness and strength of personality; it is also to understand all the music of his successors more clearly, and therefore to find ourselves enjoying later music more because of our better understanding.

The exact date of Haydn's birth is not known, but it was either the 31st March or 1st April, 1732. Haydn often gave the 31st March as his birthday, but he explained that he had really been born on the 1st April, and that his younger brother, Michael, told everyone that the earlier day was the right one to save Joseph from being called an April Fool. He was born in Rohrau, a small market town on the borders of Austria and Hungary, and not far from the frontier of what then was called Bohemia but which is now part of Czechoslovakia. His father, Mathias, was a wheelwright and wagon builder; he was a man of some importance in Rohrau, because for twenty-two years he was its *Marktrichter*, which literally means 'market magistrate'. He had to supervise the town market, see that the roads were kept in order and that the people paid their dues to the Lord of the Manor, behaved themselves properly and attended church on Sunday. But an important man in a town like Rohrau could still be poor, and when Beethoven, who had been befriended by Haydn, was shown a picture of the cottage in which Haydn was born he said, 'It seems strange that such a great man should come from such a poor cottage.'

In Rohrau, people of Austrian, Hungarian, German and Bohemian descent all mixed together, for the Austrian Empire was a great melting pot of races. Mathias and his wife Anna, a cook in the local manor house, came of German ancestry. Neither of them had any musical education, nor much education of any kind, but Mathias loved folk songs, played the harp by ear and used his harp to accompany himself when he sang. Both parents soon noticed that Joseph, who was the eldest of their children, was an unusually musical boy. He did not, like Mozart, play the harpsichord when he was four and compose minuets at five—there was no harpsichord for him to play, and no one to teach him—but he listened with delight to his father's songs and by the time he was five he could sing many of them himself. The neighbours, too, noticed how he enjoyed music, and both Mathias and Anna began to hope that he would get on in the world and work with his brain instead of his hands. Mathias believed that his son might be lucky enough to become a teacher, but Anna's hopes soared even higher and she felt that he might even rise to be a priest if only he were given some chance of a good education.

Joseph's first chance came on a Sunday in 1738. Johann Mathias Franck, who had married Mathias's half-sister, visited the Haydn cottage at Rohrau. Franck was the headmaster of the school at Hainburg, a small unimportant town which nevertheless seemed immeasurably greater and grander than Rohrau, near Pressburg but still on the Austrian side of the frontier. He was organist and director of music at the chief church there, and it seemed to Mathias and Anna that he was capable of giving their clever son the beginnings of the education he needed.

As the visit took place on a Sunday, when there was no work, the Haydn family sat down and sang their favourite songs to Mathias's harp accompaniment. Joseph joined in those he knew, and Franck at once noticed his 'weak but pleasant voice' (that is how Haydn himself described it in 1776, when he was asked for autobiographical details about himself to be included in *Das gelehrte Oesterreich*, a sort of Austrian *Who's Who*). At the same time, the six-year-old boy pretended to accompany the singing on an imaginary violin, drawing a piece of wood, representing the bow, across his left arm, which he held in the position of a player holding a violin. What was more to the point, Franck noticed, was that the 'bow' kept perfect time. He realized that he was looking at a talented child who would benefit from a musical education. Probably he realized too that if Joseph went to live in his house and attend his school, Mathias would pay for his son's keep; Franck was an important man in Hainburg, but he was badly paid and needed any extra money he could find.

So in 1738, Joseph left home for good to be a pupil at the school in Hainburg and a paying guest in Franck's house. As he passed through the gates into the little city, he must have fancied himself in a new world. Hainburg lies in a part of the Danube valley where thickly wooded hills slope down steeply towards the river. Near to the town, surrounded by meadows, tower the ruins of Hainburg Castle, where Attila the Hun, the terror of the fifth century, is said to have stayed. The boy's artistic and intellectual appetites must have been awakened by the picturesque, romantic scenery, the beautiful, fanciful façades of baroque buildings and the fascinating church of St. Philip and St. James where Franck was in charge of the music, which was sung every Sunday to the accompaniment of what must have been the first small orchestra that Joseph Haydn ever heard.

But the child soon found that even in so marvellous a city, the first real city he had ever seen, there were things to make him unhappy. He had left his mother and father behind, and knew that he would rarely see them again although Mathias made his way to Hainburg on Corpus Christi day in 1738, to attend the Guild Service there as a member of the Wheelwright's guild. Settling down in a new home among strangers was difficult enough, but Schoolmaster Franck must have added to Joseph's unhappiness. He seems to have been the same sort of teacher as Mr. Squeers, in Dickens's *Nicholas Nickleby*; his teaching method was to beat knowledge into his pupils with what he called his 'tingling rod'. On several occasions he was rebuked by the authorities for neglecting his duties, and on another he got into trouble for gambling with loaded dice.

Franck's house, too, was an unhappy place for his young lodger. Frau Franck was not a good cook or household manager, as was Joseph's mother; everything in the new home seemed grubby and disordered. His appearance was neglected, and this seems to have distressed him even more than having too little food, and that unpleasant, to eat. Many years later, when he was an old man honoured throughout Europe, he told the story of his childhood to his first biographers, Georg August Griesinger and Albert Christoph Dies, remembering the feeling of shame that neglect gave him. 'I couldn't help noticing, much to my distress,' he said, 'that I was gradually getting rather dirty, and though I thought rather highly of my little person, I wasn't always able to avoid getting stains on my clothes, and I was dreadfully ashamed of them. In fact, I became a regular little ragamuffin.'

Hainburg had its unpleasant aspects, but Joseph was beginning to make real progress as a musician. During his first year in Hainburg he learnt to read and write, and he had lessons in singing and in almost every string and wind instrument. 'Even in my sixth year,' he explained in the little sketch of his career which he wrote in 1776, 'I was able to sing some masses in the organ loft and to play a little on the harpsichord and the violin.' School began every morning at seven o'clock, with three hours of lessons—reading, writing, arithmetic and music—before Mass, after which there was a break until after dinner, at midday. Then there were three more hours of school in the afternoon. Apart from the hours of lessons and musical instruction, young Haydn was also kept busy preparing for the religious and municipal festivals in which the schoolchildren were expected to take part; the music for these had to be prepared and rehearsed. Because there were so many religious festivities, the boy must have become familiar with the Catholic church music of the period while he was still very young.

When Joseph was seven, Franck's drummer fell ill only a day or two before a procession through the city. There was no time to find a replacement, so that the small boy, after practising for two days on an improvised drum made out of a large basket covered with a cloth, became drummer for the procession. He was too small to carry the instrument, so it was strapped on to the back of a dwarf and he walked behind, solemnly beating it. The procession was a religious one, but it must have been hard for the onlookers to take it as solemnly as did the diminutive drummer. Actually, Haydn's ability to play percussion instruments amazed orchestral players long afterwards, and when, as an elderly celebrity, he gave concerts in London, he astonished the members of the orchestra by showing exactly how he wanted a particular drum passage played.

Haydn remembered some unpleasant times at Hainburg, but all through his life he also remembered how important to him Franck's teaching had been. Long after he had left the little city, he wrote, 'I have to honour this man [Franck], even though he is long dead, for teaching me so many different things, even though I got more thrashings than food in the process.'

Young Joseph had been at school in Hainburg for nearly two years when he had a great stroke of luck. Karl Georg Reutter, the newly appointed choirmaster of St. Stephen's Cathedral, Vienna, visited the town during a tour in search of new choirboys. In Hainburg, he was advised to listen to little Haydn. Joseph was sent for and given a tune to sing at sight; Reutter was surprised and delighted at the boy's ability to sing it, his enthusiasm and the purity of his tone. Reutter soon found that young Haydn was a quick learner, for when he asked the boy to sing a trill, Joseph replied, 'I don't know how to do that. My cousin [he meant Franck] cannot sing a trill, so he hasn't been able to teach me.'

Reutter showed him how a trill was sung, and after only one demonstration Joseph sang a perfect trill; Reutter was so delighted that he filled the child's pocket with the bowl of cherries he had been eating and made up his mind at once that Joseph must join his choir. Vienna was much further than Hainburg from Rohrau, but when Mathias and Anna were asked to send the boy to Reutter's choir school, they realized that their clever son was being offered an opportunity of getting on in the world and agreed that he should go to Vienna as soon as he reached his eighth birthday.

Impatient for his new life, Haydn practised singing scales to develop his voice. All through his life he was a man of great determination and ambition, and this he showed them during his time of waiting to leave Franck, so he made good progress. At last it was time for him to leave Hainburg and to continue his education as a choirboy in Vienna, the splendid glittering capital of the Austrian Empire. Members of the *Wiener Sängerknaben*, the world-famous 'Vienna Boys' Choir', can look back to Haydn as one of the great men—Schubert was another—who preceded them and undertook many of the duties which they still perform.

II

St. Stephen's, Vienna

Vienna and the city's surroundings were more enchanting than Joseph had ever dared expect; he fell in love with the city and remained in love with it for the rest of his life. But he soon found out that there was a bleaker side of life, as there had been in Hainburg. The choirmaster, Georg Reutter, turned out to be a character very similar to his previous master, Franck. He said, many years later, that he found Reutter to be a harsh, cruel and unfeeling man who had never given him more than two lessons in composition. In fact, his only cause for remembering Reutter was that 'he had promised me special tuition but gave me nothing except a great deal of harsh treatment'.

Haydn received no help or encouragement in his childish attempts at composition. He had tried to write a piece in twelve parts, thinking that the page must only be filled with plenty of notes to be good music. Reutter laughed when he looked at the boy's effort: 'Oh you stupid boy,' he scoffed, 'aren't two parts enough for you?' But he made no attempt to show Haydn how the two parts should be arranged.

Once again Joseph became a small, ragged and underfed urchin. Sometimes the choir gave recitals in the grand houses of the Viennese nobility, and it was only after these recitals, when the singers were given refreshments, that the choirboys had enough to eat. Haydn said later that during this time he found these recitals very attractive: 'My love for such concerts was so great that I tried to sing as beautifully as I could in order to be invited as a skilled performer.' But the prospect of extra food meant as much to him as the music.

The boys worked hard. Apart from such private concerts, they took part in court ceremonies and civic ceremonies, at concerts at court and sometimes in the open-air music which was one of the delights of pleasure-loving Vienna. But their chief duty was to sing High Mass every morning and Vespers every afternoon in the cathedral; on all the greater feast days, the

19

music was specially elaborate and needed extra rehearsal. The choir had a huge repertory, but it was always being enlarged by new Italian and Austrian compositions written with brilliant orchestral accompaniments. It included, too, many of the more austere, unaccompanied masterpieces of earlier composers; there were also marriages and funerals to be attended to. The amount of music to be learnt—for concerts, public ceremonies and special services were usually occasions for new works—seems not to have worried Joseph at all, and in many ways so much music to learn must have been good training, helping a would-be composer to make up for Reutter's neglect.

But, naturally enough, young Joseph was not always on his best behaviour during these outings. The choir visited the Empress Maria Theresa at her newly built palace, Schönbrunn, and the sight of the scaffolding, which had not yet been removed, was too great a temptation. With yells of delight the small boys began to swing and clamber up the wooden structure. Before long the Empress herself appeared at the window and shouted furiously that she would have them all thrashed if she caught anyone playing there again. The following day Joseph couldn't resist showing off to his friends and alone climbed to the top of the scaffolding. Once again the Empress appeared at the window and demanded that Haydn should be beaten for his disobedience. Reutter only too willingly obeyed the command.

From 1745 onwards things became steadily worse for Joseph. As he grew older he was no longer able to sing the high notes the younger boys could reach with such ease. This became more noticeable when Joseph's brother Michael joined the choir. Michael, who was then eight years old, had a wonderful soprano voice and, together with his ability to learn very quickly, he shone more brightly than Joseph had ever done.

Michael delighted the Empress so much with his singing that she gave him a present of twenty-four golden ducats. Joseph was now overshadowed by his younger brother and, as if this humiliation wasn't enough, the Empress complained to Reutter: 'The elder Haydn boy sings like a crow.'

It was now obvious to Reutter that Joseph was no longer of any use and he at once began to look for an excuse to get rid of him. But Joseph seems to have been unaware that his days in the choir of St. Stephen's were nearly at an end, for he very soon gave Reutter the opportunity he had been waiting for.

Haydn had been annoyed by one of the other choirboys, who, unlike the rest, wore his long hair in a pigtail. During choir-practice he sat behind the boy and had his revenge by leaning forward and cutting off the pigtail with

Above, the village of Rohrau where Haydn was born in 1732; *below*, the entry of Haydn's birth in the parish register of Rohrau church

An engraving of St. Stephen's, Vienna

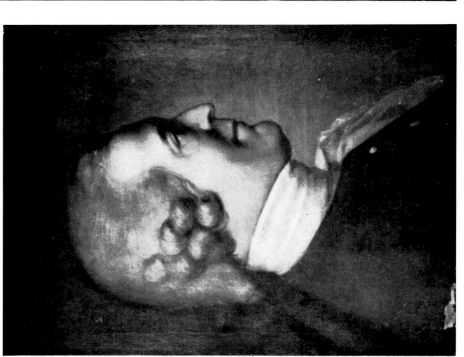

Georg Reutter the kapellmeister at St. Stephen's
Cathedral, Vienna

a pair of scissors. But Joseph's victory was short-lived for he was immediately summoned to Reutter's office. Feeling that a beating was rather beneath his dignity, Haydn tried to avoid the inevitable punishment by saying that he would rather leave at once than be beaten. This was more than Reutter had hoped for and he replied: 'That won't help you—first you will be whipped and then off you go!'

On a bitter November day in 1749, Joseph, with three worn shirts, a ragged jacket and no money, was turned out into the world to fend for himself.

III

'Making Something Out of Nothing'

As he wandered along the streets Haydn could think of no one to turn to in Vienna. It might have crossed his mind to take the road for Rohrau, but his mother was still anxious that he should enter the Church. If he went back to his parents, he might be forced to give up composing, and that thought probably made him determined to stay in Vienna.

Joseph tried desperately to think of somewhere to shelter for the night. Just as he was giving up all hope he had the luck to meet Michael Spangler, a poor singer and music teacher whom he knew by sight. On hearing of the young composer's misfortunes, Spangler insisted Haydn should share the garret where he lived with his wife and small son.

Although he was grateful to have a roof over his head, after several months Spangler's second son was born, and Haydn knew he could no longer continue his serious studies in such cramped conditions. Shortly after deciding to leave, Joseph had a stroke of good luck. Anton Buchholz, a tradesman friend and colleague of Haydn's father, decided to help the composer by lending him, unconditionally, one hundred and fifty florins. The sum must have seemed enormous to Joseph at that moment, for he was penniless. He immediately moved into the cheapest room available. He never forgot the generous loan and in his will left the tradesman's granddaughter one hundred florins: '. . . in my youth her grandfather lent me one hundred and fifty florins when I greatly needed them, a debt which, however, I repaid fifty years ago'.

It was the custom in those days for poor and socially unacceptable people to live on the top floors of houses. Haydn's new lodgings were little better than the ones he had just left. He rented a gloomy, uncomfortable attic at 1220 St. Michael's Square, Vienna, with no fire and a roof which let in the rain, but with a decrepit old harpsichord—he described it as 'worm-eaten'—which he managed to buy.

At least Joseph was able to earn a poor living and to continue composing, and at this time, about 1750, it is probable that he wrote his first mass, *Mass in F*.

Every morning at half past six, he played the violin at a monastery High Mass, hurried from there to play at Mass in the private chapel of a nobleman, Count Haugwitz, and made his way from that to the cathedral, where he sang in the choir as a tenor. The rest of the day passed in teaching, composition and practice until the evening, when he often played again as one of the orchestra at a nobleman's private concert or, if nothing else was available, in one of the parties of musicians who made a little money playing in the streets. He arranged a good deal of music for the odd combinations of instruments which made up such serenade parties.

At the same time, Haydn realized his poor knowledge of musical theory could be heard in his compositions, and to overcome this he began long hours of study. The works which most impressed him were the keyboard sonatas of Carl Philip Emanuel Bach, one of the sons of the great composer Johann Sebastian Bach who had died in 1750. He remarked about these works, which were in a new, very emotional, serious, expressive style, 'I didn't leave the clavier until I had mastered them all. I played them many times for my own delight, especially when I felt oppressed and discouraged.'

As well as these serious studies, Haydn composed several pieces for amusement and relaxation. One piece, written for three instruments, was performed by Joseph and two friends in the streets, as was the custom in Vienna at that time. The trio happened to play beneath the window of a famous comedian, Kurz Bernardon. The comedian was at once attracted by the originality of the music and invited Haydn into his house. Several minutes later Joseph left carrying the libretto of an opera entitled *Der krumme Teufel* ('The Limping Devil'), which Bernardon had just completed. Within days he had written the music, and the comedy-opera became a great success until a nobleman decided that the composer and librettist had written it to make fun of him, and prohibited performances of the opera.

Joseph heard that the great Italian writer and poet, Pietro Metastasio, who was the author of a large number of very popular opera 'libretti' (as the books which contain the words of operas are called) lived on the third floor of the same rickety building and when he also learned that the poet had a small girl in his care, and that she was anxious to have music lessons, he realized that this was an opportunity not to be missed. At once he offered his services as a teacher and was gladly accepted.

This led to another meeting which helped him. It was arranged that his young pupil should take singing lessons from Niccolo Porpora, the much-admired composer of vocal music. Haydn acted as accompanist during each lesson and came to know Porpora quite well. He realized he could learn a great deal about theory and technique from the master, who was an old man of seventy. Before long Joseph asked if he might become his assistant. Porpora agreed to the idea and took Haydn to a fashionable summer resort where they were to give music lessons.

Joseph served his new master diligently, cleaning shoes, brushing clothes and was prepared to put up with occasional cuffs as long as Porpora would correct his compositions. While he struggled in this lowly position his brother, Michael, was having far more impressive success. Just as he had outshone Joseph in the choir at St. Stephen's he was now engaged as conductor to the Bishop of Grosswardein.

Instead of depressing Joseph, the news of his brother's success only strengthened his determination to compose. Years later, when his music was well known, he wrote: 'Young people can learn from my example that something can come out of nothing. What I have become is all the result of dire need.'

Because he was Porpora's assistant, Haydn began gradually to mix with the nobility. These were the only people in eighteenth-century Vienna able to help a young composer.

It was during one of the social gatherings to which Porpora introduced him that Haydn met Karl Joseph von Fürnberg, an ardent lover of music. Shortly after, he was invited to von Fürnberg's country house to take part in a performance of chamber music. Haydn was thrilled, for at last he seemed to be making real progress.

The house was situated amongst rolling hills from where one could see high mountains in the distance. It was during his stay that Joseph wrote the first string quartets. They were received with such enthusiasm that he was inspired to write more.

Due to these first successes, Haydn's position and reputation as a composer began to prosper. Encouraged by this, he would often work for sixteen to eighteen hours a day, composing and giving lessons to his increasing number of pupils.

Von Fürnberg realized that a man of Haydn's genius should be helped as much as possible. Although reluctant to lose the composer from his household, in 1758 von Fürnberg recommended Haydn to Count Ferdinand Maximilian von Morzin of Bohemia. The proposal was accepted and Haydn became the Count's *Capellmeister*, or music director at Lukavec, the Count's country seat. This was a great step forward for Joseph both socially and financially, for not only was he now paid two hundred florins a year, as well as receiving free board and lodging, but the Count had his own orchestra of sixteen musicians who played, during the winter, in Vienna and during the summer in Lukaveč. Haydn had to organize all the music which the Count's orchestra was to perform and it was during the summer months that his first symphony was composed and performed.

Haydn conducted from the harpsichord, as was the tradition. There was loud applause at the end of the symphony, but he was unaware that among the audience was Prince Paul Anton Esterházy, a nobleman of enormous wealth and with vast estates. He took care to remember the name of the young composer whose symphony he had just enjoyed.

For the first time in his life, Haydn could think himself financially secure, so he at once planned to marry. He had fallen in love with one of his pupils, Therese Keller, whose father was a barber in Vienna. Keller had helped Haydn in the composer's bad days, and the composer was both fond of his benefactor and grateful to him. When Therese became a nun, Haydn wrote his Organ Concerto in C for the ceremony at which she took her vows (or he claimed, much later in life, to have done so; some scholars believe that the Organ Concerto was written earlier) and, to please her father, proposed to her elder sister Maria, who accepted him. The two were married, apparently, in 1760. Maria Keller seems to have been unattractive both in appearance and in character; she was bad-tempered and had no interest whatever in her husband's work nor in his growing fame in the years that followed. The marriage was unhappy and, to Haydn's great grief, the two had no children.

It was not long before Haydn's hard-won security seemed to evaporate. Count Morzin ran into financial difficulties and had to discharge his musicians, so that Haydn was again unemployed. But before his situation became desperate, Prince Paul Anton Esterházy offered him a post. The Esterházy *Capellmeister*, Gregorious Werner, was growing old—he had been in charge of the music of the Esterházy family for thirty-two years—and his style was too old-fashioned to please the Prince, who had just retired from a diplomatic career in Italy and who was now eager to build up the musical establishment he had inherited. He sent his best violinist, Tomasini, and his best tenor to study in Italy; he had brought back a large collection of new Italian music with him, and, because he had fallen in love with Italian opera, he ordered the building of an opera house at his summer palace in Eisenstadt. Prince Paul Anton was not simply a music-lover; he was an intelligent, very cultured man who played both the violin and the cello respectably.

The post he offered to Haydn was that of assistant *Capellmeister* to Werner. Werner would continue to be responsible for the Prince's church music, but Haydn would take charge of everything else. Provided that he gave satisfaction the newcomer could expect to succeed to Werner's post when it fell vacant. Haydn—though neither he nor Prince Paul Anton knew it—had found his life's work.

IV

Vienna and Eisenstadt

Like any other nobleman of the Empire, Prince Paul Anton spent his winters in Vienna and his summers at Eisenstadt, where his palace was built on his country estate on a scale suitable to one of the wealthiest of European princes. At Eisenstadt there were more than two hundred guest rooms, a picture gallery and a theatre even before the building of the opera house began. His orchestra, when Haydn joined him, seems to have consisted of eleven or twelve string players, a flautist, two oboists, two bassoonists, two horn players and a timpanist. Two violinists and a cellist made up the orchestra for services in the chapel, there were trumpeters and drummers in the Prince's regiment, and all these musicians could be brought together for special occasions. Eisenstadt had its own small band of town musicians, and they too could be added to the court musicians if they were needed. The singers of the Prince's choir were also at Haydn's disposal for music outside the chapel. With an accomplished musician, eager to hear up-to-date, original music as his patron and these forces at his command, Haydn had a splendid opportunity.

He was twenty-nine and had survived several years of great hardship. Georg August Griesinger, who wrote one of the first biographies of Haydn and collected the necessary facts in conversations with him, described him in detail. 'He was small, but sturdy and strongly built. His forehead was broad and well-modelled, his eyes bright and fiery, his other features full and strongly marked, and his whole appearance and bearing suggested prudence and quiet gravity.' Another biographer who knew him, Albert Christoph Dies, wrote that, like those of many small men, his legs were too short to be in proper proportion to his body. Dies too mentions the fiery look of Haydn's eyes, but says that in spite of it his look was 'moderate and kind'. Like many—perhaps the majority—of eighteenth-century people, he had suffered from smallpox, and the disease had marked his face. He had a 'hawk-like' nose.

In many ways his education was very lop-sided. In later years his faithful copyist tells us he read for an hour every day; but at this time his reading was mostly about music. He had a thorough grounding in Latin and corrected Fux's famous textbook, *Gradus ad Parnassum*, in Latin; he spoke Italian fluently and a little French; later he spoke English tolerably well. He spoke German with a noticeable provincial accent of the sort that cultured Viennese found picturesque, as educated people would find the speech of an English celebrity who never learnt to drop a west-country or northern accent. But his quickness of mind and shrewdness showed in many ways all through his life. When, later, publishers were eager to bring out editions of his music and make a profit from his fame, he realized at once that they would exploit him if they could; a great deal of his music had been published without his permission (people speak of such unofficial editions as 'pirated') and had brought him no money. He soon found ways of exploiting the publishers who intended to make money out of him. The notebooks he kept during his two visits to London show how fascinated he was by new scenes, new knowledge, new ideas and a new way of life although he was fifty-eight before he left Austria.

All his life he was a very devout Catholic who seems never to have doubted or questioned his faith. All his bigger works are headed *In nomine Domini* ('In the Name of the Lord') and at the end of each he wrote *Laus Deo* ('Praise be to God'). His faith was, to him, a source of happiness, and when someone accused him of setting the final section of the Mass ('O Lamb of God, that takest away the sins of the world, have mercy upon us') to music that is too cheerful to be appropriate, he replied that to him the important words of that prayer are not 'sins' but 'takest away', so that the thought made him happy. Religion made him humble; he would have been stupid if he had not realized how great his gifts were, but to him they were simply gifts for which he thanked God, and when one of the fans who always surround successful artists told him that he should be granted a palace with splendid gardens, a coach and horses and the great men of the world to be his companions, he simply replied that splendour would not suit him. 'I had a hard time when I was young,' he said, 'but now I have a comfortable house, three or four courses for dinner every day and a good glass of wine. I can afford to dress decently and to hire a coach whenever I need one. I have met kings and emperors who have said flattering things to me, but I wouldn't choose such people for friends. I prefer friends of my own station.'

He loved hunting and fishing, but he never became a good horseman. He

A high mass in St. Stephen's, Vienna

The title-page and last page of Haydn's comic opera *The Limping Devil*

CHORUS.

Alle. Wahre Lieb sucht alle Gänge,
Alle Vortheil, alle List,
Bis der Gegner in die Länge,
Endlich doch betrogen ist.

Bernardon.
Gleich und gleich gehört zusammen.

Siamenta.
Gleich, und gleich liebt jedermann,
O das sind die schönsten Flammen,
Die die Tugend zündet an.

Alle. Wahre Lieb sucht alle Gänge,
Alle Vortheil, alle List,
Biß der Gegner in die Länge,
Endlich doch betrogen ist.

ENDE.

NB. die Musique sowohl von der Opera-Comique,
als auch der Pantomime ist componiret
Von
Herrn Joseph Heyden.

Der neue
Krumme Teufel.
Eine
OPERA-COMIQUE
von zwey Aufzügen;
Nebst einer
Kinder-Pantomime,
Betitult:
ARLEQUIN
Der neue Abgott Ram
in America.

Alles componiret
Von Joseph Kurz.

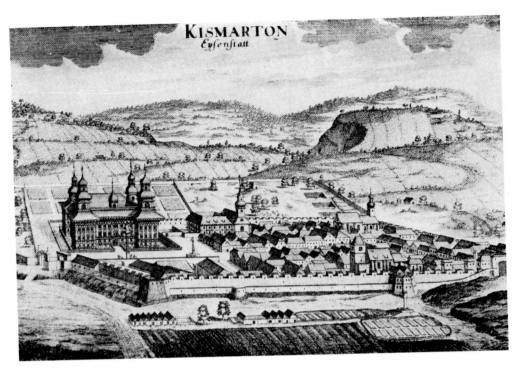

Two engravings: (*above*) the town of Eisenstadt and (*below*) the Esterházy Palace
at Eisenstadt

had no opportunity to learn to ride until he went to Lukaveč as Count Morzin's *Capellmeister*, and once he had fallen off a horse he was unwilling to try to ride again. But one day he shot three hazel hens which were served for dinner to the Empress Maria Theresa when she stayed at the Prince's new palace at Eszterhása, and he was very proud of having done so.

'A harmless roguery—what the British call *humour*—was one of Haydn's outstanding characteristics,' wrote Griesinger. 'He easily and by preference discovered the comic side of anything.' This is something the listener discovers as he concentrates on Haydn's music. Haydn wrote much serious, deep, sorrowful and sometimes angry music—he was far too intelligent and sensitive to believe that life is simply a joke, and he himself experienced unhappiness, but often his sense of humour takes charge of the music. Sometimes he makes orchestral jokes like the great crash which interrupts the gentle little tune of the slow movement of the *Surprise Symphony*. But much more often Haydn's humour, especially in finales, is simply an irresistible outburst of high spirits which dazzle the listener by their inventiveness; for Haydn, when he discovers the 'comic side' of anything, is as intelligent and as inventive as he is when he is meditating solemnly on some deeply serious subject.

Another of his outstanding characteristics was a passion for order. Everything about him—the house he lived in and the manuscripts he wrote— were tidy. The little boy who felt ashamed when he was allowed to grow shabby and grubby from neglect grew up to be man who always dressed formally to receive visitors, even when he was a frail old man in his seventies. It was kind of people to visit him, he thought, so he was determined to repay their kindness with his own courtesy.

Haydn's sense of order, like his humour, is in his music. When he wrote his first symphonies, there were several forms in which he could work, all used by composers for the same sort of lively, easy-going, entertaining music. Haydn set them all into order by distinguishing their real characters. The symphony, he realized, would make stronger, more logical, more dramatic music than the serenade and the divertimento, both of which he used as a young man for cheerful, good-natured but not specially profound or ambitious work. The string quartet, which had always been used as though its four instruments were a miniature orchestra without special qualities of their own, became in Haydn's work a form which depended on the very similar qualities of tone of the four instruments and on the idea that a string quartet is not written for a solo violin with an accompaniment by another violin, a viola and a cello but on the equality of the four as partners in the music. Haydn did not theorize about these things; he was simply a great composer who instinctively realized the inner nature of the musical forms he knew and established an order among them through his compositions.

But in 1761, when he signed a contract to become Prince Paul Anton's Assistant *Capellmeister*, this was all in the future. We do not know how much of Haydn's music, apart from the early symphonies which he had heard at Lukaveč, the Prince had managed to track down before he offered the composer a post, or whether Haydn was simply the best unemployed composer he could find to carry out the task of building up Esterházy music. The early symphonies have vigour and invention but only the promise of the greatness Haydn had not yet shown.

Haydn's contract with Prince Paul Anton was more or less the same as that offered to any court musician. Werner was to remain in charge of the music in the Prince's chapel, but Haydn was to be responsible for all the music for court entertainment. As a member of the Prince's household he had to set a good example to the musicians subordinate to him and, for the sake of discipline, to avoid 'any undue familiarity' with them. It was his duty to compose whatever the Prince commanded, and the works he composed would become the Prince's property; he was not to distribute extra copies of them or to allow other people to have copies of them without Paul Anton's special permission, and he was not allowed to compose music for anyone else unless he were given permission to do so.

Socially, he ranked with liveried servants like the Prince's major domo, his wine steward or the two court painters. As his fame grew, he became friendly with the very superior class of 'House Officers' who managed the Prince's estates and finances, in spite of the rigid class distinctions of the court. Though he was never made a nobleman, it became customary as he grew famous for people to refer to him as 'Herr von Haydn', the German 'von' being an indication of nobility which he had never officially received.

Every morning and afternoon, dressed in court livery and wearing his wig, he had to go to the Prince's antechamber to receive instructions. He was to settle any disputes among the musicians and refer them to the Prince only if he could not deal with them himself. It was his duty to see that the instruments and music library were kept in order (he tuned the keyboard instruments himself), to train the female singers and to keep himself in practice on all the instruments he played. The contract left a lot of details to be taken for granted—daily rehearsals with the orchestra and, perhaps, the singers, seeing that new works were correctly copied when instrumental parts were made from them, and so on. In return, he was paid 400 gulden (about £40) a year. His uniform was provided for him, and so was his board, which was reckoned at half a gulden a day. In the course of time, his salary rose to 782 gulden. This amount could buy far more in Haydn's lifetime than it can buy now, and it is worth while remembering that the village parson, in Goldsmith's poem *The Deserted Village*, was, in the eyes of his parishioners, 'passing rich with forty pounds a year'.

Haydn's contract ran for three years from 1st May 1761. If he did not wish it to be renewed he was to say so six months before it expired, so that the Prince would have reasonable time in which to replace him. He could be dismissed without any notice from Paul Anton if his work was not satisfactory, but if the Prince was pleased with him he could expect to succeed to Werner's post when it fell vacant.

The first Symphonies which he wrote for his new Patron were a cycle, *Le Matin, Le Midi*, and *Le Soir et La Tempesta* (Nos. 6, 7 and 8). Perhaps to please his new orchestra, Haydn included passages for solo violins in *Le Matin*, and for two violins and cello in *Le Midi*. *Le Soir* ends with a movement which has its own title, *La Tempesta*. In his first years as Assistant *Capellmeister*, Haydn wrote five violin concertos, a Cello Concerto in C which was lost until the 1960s, a Double Bass Concerto and two Horn Concertos. The Concerto seems not to have been a favourite form of his—later in life he wrote concertos only when they were expressly commissioned—so probably the early works were written to please his orchestra. He was extremely busy at this time, and when he wrote out the score of the first Horn Concerto he mixed up the staves of the oboe and the first violin and wrote on the score, as he corrected his mistake, 'Written while asleep.'

New musicians and new singers were engaged in accordance with Paul Anton's policy of modernizing and expanding the Esterházy music, but before his ambitions could bear any fruit he died, to be succeeded by his brother, Prince Nicolaus. Nicolaus was an extremely cultured man, passionately interested in science, literature and music. People called him 'the Magnificent' for the splendour in which he lived, comparing him to Lorenzo the Magnificent the greatest of the Medici family which ruled Florence in its greatest days. Like Lorenzo, Nicolaus was a generous and understanding patron of the arts, capable, at most times, of remembering that people as humble as musicians were really human.

For the celebrations at which Prince Nicolaus succeeded to his title in 1762, Haydn wrote, rehearsed and performed four Italian operas at high speed. By 1765, he had composed most of the concertos described above,

Sonata in C for Harpsichord or Clavichord

Allegro moderato

Menuet

Trio

C

Menuet da Capo

FINALE
Allegro

about thirty symphonies, the early string quartets (now known as opus 1 and opus 2, but the early collections were not made by Haydn), a large number of piano trios and piano sonatas written mostly for his aristocratic pupils in the Esterházy family, and various odds and ends. In addition to this, Prince Nicolaus played an already old-fashioned instrument called the baryton, a development of the old viola da gamba which was rested on the player's knees and was extremely difficult to play (perhaps that is why Prince Nicolaus preferred it). Naturally, not a great deal of music was written for it, so that Haydn had to compose a great deal of music for the Prince to play.

There are divertimenti for baryton, violin and cello, duets for two barytons and sonatas for baryton and cello. In the 1770s, the Prince's delight in
his strange instrument seemed to decrease, but until then Haydn had provided him with a vast amount of music—there are a hundred and twenty-
five divertimenti and twelve other works. He had to teach himself to play
the instrument so that he could join in the six duets for two barytons, and
the Prince had always to have the more difficult part.

This seems to be a part of his work which he did not always enjoy. One
of the divertimenti is headed 'written to order', but the baryton set him
interesting musical problems and more often than not this aspect of the
compositions appealed to him. The Prince believed that a baryton could be
played in only a few keys, chiefly those in which its strings were tuned.
Haydn, having secretly taught himself the instrument, played to the Prince
in all sorts of keys. The Prince listened unmoved (to show emotion would
not have been princely) and, at the end, simply said, 'Haydn, that is something *you* have to know about.' For a moment the composer was hurt, but
he said, 'I reminded myself that I had harvested a certain fame not as a
practising virtuoso but as a *Capellmeister*, and I was ashamed that I had
neglected composing for half a year and at once threw myself into it with
renewed vigour.'

All this activity makes the letter which Prince Nicolaus wrote to Haydn
in 1765 difficult to understand. Werner had complained to the Prince about
his Assistant *Capellmeister* that Haydn, whose music seemed to him strange
and affected, had no control over the musicians because he was too friendly
with them, and that, in consequence, many of them were neglecting their
duties, not turning up for the duties in the chapel and behaving so carelessly
that the collection of church music was in complete disorder. The Prince at
once wrote to rebuke Haydn, ordered him to see that players were always
present to do their duty, that the church music library should be put into
order and that he should compose more music instead of wasting his time.
With this dressing down, he included a demand for more baryton works;
when he got them, he gave Haydn a present over and above his salary for
them; perhaps his letter only meant that, when a superior complained
about one of his subordinates, the superior's word simply had to be taken.

In 1766, Werner died and Haydn was appointed to his post, which, of
course, meant that he now had to compose church music and see that performances in the Prince's chapel were up to standard; this meant not only
more composition but more rehearsals and more teaching to be done. But
by this time, Prince Nicolaus had changed the way of life of his entire court.

He disliked Vienna as much as Haydn loved the city, and Eisenstadt did not seem to appeal to him. A shooting lodge at Eszterháza, deep in the Hungarian marshes and miles from anywhere, had become a great palace, second only, people said, to the French king's palace at Versailles. The landscape was flat and uneventful; to build on it, marshes had to be drained (the local agriculture benefited a great deal) and materials brought from far away, but by 1766 the new palace was ready for occupation.

A watermark taken from paper used by Haydn.
The chapters which follow give a selection
of these watermarks

V

Eszterháza

Eszterháza dwarfed the splendour of Eisenstadt. Here Prince Nicolaus had a marionette theatre and an opera house as well as his picture gallery. Everyone connected with the palace had to live somewhere in its buildings, and the musicians had a house of their own in which Haydn had married quarters but most of his orchestra and choir had room only for themselves. There was a chapel and its staff of clergy; the Prince had his own doctors, with a separate medical staff for his underlings and a hospital building in which they could be treated. An army of servants, carefully graded in rigidly observed classes, was needed to maintain what was really a world of its own in which there was no one to worry the Prince except those he cared to invite to share his glories. But its isolation was so great that even Dr. Charles Burney, the English historian of music who toured the Continent to gather materials for his work between 1770 and 1772, did not move so far off the beaten track though he was a passionate admirer of Haydn's music and a very determined traveller.

As an old man, Haydn realized that Eszterháza had done a great deal for him. 'Not only did I have the encouragement of constant approval,' he said, 'but as conductor of the orchestra I could experiment, find out what made a good effect and what weakened it, so I was free to alter, improve, add or omit and be as bold as I pleased. Cut off from the world I had no one to bother me and I was forced to become original.'

But he did not always enjoy his isolation. He was cut off from the world with a wife who meant nothing to him and to whom he meant nothing, unable to make musical friends, for his contract forbade him to do so, and both his concentration on his work and his specialized education meant that he had few interests outside his art; without musical friends he was bound to be lonely. In Vienna he had friends who shared his interests, but he saw Vienna less often as the Prince grew more reluctant to leave the lonely splendour of Eszterháza, where he spent more time each year. He went to

Vienna only to pay his respects to the Court at Christmas-time. As it turned out, the musicians often stayed in Hungary from the middle of February to shortly before Christmas. This long stay at Eszterháza produced one of Haydn's most famous works, the so-called *Farewell* Symphony.

In the late autumn of 1772, the musicians thought they had stayed long enough in the icy marshes of Hungary, and they appealed to Haydn to help them. Haydn knew that the way to the Prince's heart was through music, so he wrote what at first appeared to be a normal four-movement symphony, but in the very strange key of F sharp minor (nobody has ever written another symphony in that key). The last movement is very fast but suddenly grinds to a halt and a long slow movement begins. Then the musicians started a curious procedure. Each played, alone or in a small group, a solo, after which he blew out his candle, collected his instrument, and left. One after another the orchestra began to disappear—the oboes, horns, bassoon, the double basses. Soon the orchestra was only a handful of violins and violas. The violas left, and then most of the violins. The stately music room was almost dark, with just Haydn and Tomasini, the Prince's best violinist, playing, their shadows casting strange shapes on the stuccoed walls. Then the piece ended, and the two final players—the leader and the princely *Capellmeister*—blew out their candles and left. The Prince and his guests were astonished, but they understood what the music was telling them; the Prince went back to the musicians and said, 'Well, if you are leaving, we might as well leave, too,' whereupon the Court departed shortly thereafter.

Perhaps it was the loneliness of these years which made Haydn find Luigia Polzelli attractive. Haydn enjoyed the company of women, and as his wife was not a companion, it was natural enough that someone should take her place. Luigia Polzelli was a soprano who, with her violinist husband, joined the Esterházy musicians in 1779. The two were only mediocre musicians, and Luigia's return for Haydn's friendship seems to have been expressed in continual demands for money. She eventually insisted that he signed an agreement declaring that if his wife died he would marry no one but her. The composer later said that he would not be bound by his promise, but although Luigia had by that time married again, he left her an annuity in his will.

During his first years at Eszterháza, Haydn's finest and most ambitious works were symphonies, and many of the most impressive were written in these years.

In many of the symphonies he wrote in his early years as Eszterházy

Capellmeister, he experimented with the orchestra. In some symphonies, like No. 13 and No. 31, he used four horns. In No. 22, which came to be called 'The Philosopher', instead of oboes he uses *cors anglais* (English horns), which play alto to the oboes' soprano and have a less bright as well as a deeper tone. In some he uses a flute, but mostly he writes for two oboes, a bassoon, two horns and strings. When the work was for some specially grand or festive occasion, he added trumpets. Because the orchestra was not yet standardized, he tried out these different combinations of instruments to find out which gave the best balance and the best effect for the sort of music each work contained.

The later 1760s and the 1770s were a time in which Haydn's style changed and deepened so profoundly that many German critics have referred to this period as his years of *Sturm und Drang* ('Storm and Stress'). His music began to marry the symphonic technique of thematic development to the older technique of counterpoint, still very much alive in the church music of the period, which plays off themes and melodies simultaneously against each other, so that the ear is listening to the progress of two or more lines of melody at the same time, and finding excitement and expressiveness in their agreements and contradictions. Haydn's new emotionalism and musical strength, though he was cut off from the world, were something he shared with the other, lesser composers of the period, but in his music they lead to more variety, more excitement and more intensity of feeling than his contemporaries could achieve.

It is not, that between 1768 and 1772, Haydn's music became tragic, though he wrote several intensely tragic symphonies during these years; the great thing is that his compositions become stronger, the joy more splendid and the sorrow more deeply moving; sometimes the music has a stern anger and fierceness, and he experiments with different types of themes. At least two of the symphonies, *Lamentatione* (No. 26, composed in 1768) and *La Passione* (No. 49, composed in the same year), are religious works—the 'Passion' he refers to is the suffering of Christ—take some of their themes from the plain-chant melodies of the Catholic Church. No. 44 (composed about 1772) is called the *Trauersinfonie* (Mourning Symphony), and while its slow movement is nobly sorrowful, the other movements, which include a gaunt minuet, are violent and angry. The *Farewell* Symphony, which won the orchestra its break from Eszterháza, sounds as though it is meant to be a joke, but its fast movements are relentlessly stormy and the 'joke' itself, in which the players depart, is a beautiful, slow, consoling postscript to a violent finale.

Slow movement from Sonata for Piano in A flat major, No. 46

(It is important to remember that Haydn's symphonies are not numbered in the order of their composition, largely because they became known to the public through their publication often by publishers who printed them without Haydn's knowledge. His own incomplete catalogue of his works was drawn up when he was an old man with an erratic memory.)

Other unconventional types of melody appear in his music at this time. Sometimes themes are borrowed from folk songs—German, Austrian, Czech or Hungarian—or based on folk-song styles, and some use Hungarian gypsy music tunes. Minuets, instead of being stately court dances, become rougher and rustic, or tough and intellectual.

The new intensity of style belongs not only to his symphonies but to everything he wrote. Six string quartets (his first for about ten years, Op. 9) were written in 1769 and six more (Op. 17) came in 1770, but these, though they are beautiful, characteristic music, seem to be only steps towards the six brilliant, sometimes gay but seriously worked out set of Op. 20 composed in 1772. These seem to have had some extremely personal meaning for Haydn. The finale of Op. 20, No. 2 is headed *Sic fugit amicus amicum* ('So a friend flies from his friend') as though it considers some betrayal of friendship, but we do not know what in Haydn's life it might apply to. Even his piano sonatas, though most were written for others to play, are deeper and more expressive after 1768, and in 1771 came the Sonata in C minor which is the finest of them up to that date.

Many of the works of the 'Storm and Stress' period are written in minor keys like the outlandish F sharp minor of the *Farewell* Symphony, and this itself tends to make them sound more thoughtful and more troubled than the earlier symphonies which had been in major keys, usually those like C major and D major in which an orchestra can sound most brilliant.

The church music he wrote between the death of Werner and 1782, when a new, reforming Emperor, Joseph II, began to discourage elaborate, orchestral music for church services, includes his setting of the hymn *Stabat Mater* in 1767; this was his finest piece of church music up to that date. The composer was allowed leave to perform it in Vienna, and a letter to the Court Secretary tells us something of the occasion:

Eisenstadt, 20th March 1768

Nobly born,
Highly respected Sir!
You will recall that last year I set to music with all my power the highly esteemed hymn called Stabat Mater, and that I sent it to the great and

world-celebrated Hasse with no other intention than that in case, here and there, I had not expressed adequately words of such great importance, this lack could be rectified by a master so successful in all forms of music. But contrary to my merits, this unique artist honoured the work by inexpressible praise, and wished nothing more than to hear it performed with the good players it requires. Since, however, there is a great want of singers *utriusque generis* [of the right kind] in Vienna, I would therefore humbly and obediently ask His Serene and Gracious Highness through you, Sir, to allow me, Weigl and his wife, and Friberth to go to Vienna next Thursday, there on Friday afternoon at the church of the Brothers of Mercy to further the honour of our gracious prince by the performance of his servant; we would return to Eisenstadt on Saturday evening.

Johann Adolph Hasse was one of the finest and most respected composers of opera in the period of Bach and Handel. He had been *Capellmeister* to the Elector of Saxony, in Dresden, from 1730 to 1760. In 1768, he was living in Vienna and trying to maintain the old principles of opera against new composers like Gluck, who were eager to reform it and make it more dramatic. The companions whom Haydn wished to take with him were a cellist married to a soprano singer in the choir; Friberth was one of its best tenors. A postcript to the letter asks the Court Secretary to assure the Prince that a new set of baryton divertimenti would be ready 'one of these next weeks'. The work was a resounding success in Vienna.

In 1773, Haydn composed two pieces of church music which soon became as well known as his *Stabat Mater*: a setting of the Latin hymn *Salve Regina* in G minor for four solo voices, solo organ and strings; and the enormous Cantata Mass—that is to say, a Mass written on a large scale with its words broken into sections some of which are turned into solo arias —written in honour of the patroness of music, the *Missa Sanctae Caeciliae* in C major, which includes some of the most magnificent and beautifully worked out fugues that Haydn ever composed.

The year before, in 1772, Haydn had written a Mass for Prince Nicolaus's name-day (that is to say, St. Nicholas's Day, 6th December; in many Catholic countries, the day of the saint after whom a person was named used to be celebrated more than an actual birthday) entitled the *Missa Sancti Nicolai*. This is a work on a smaller scale and in the pastoral spirit felt to be suitable to a Mass composed for the Christmas season. About 1775 he composed another small-scale Mass probably for the Eisenstadt chapel of the order of the Brothers of Mercy; this is the *Missa S. Joanni de Deo*, St. John of God, the patron saint of the order of the Brothers of Mercy. During the *Benedictus*, whose length was determined by the Catholic ritual at that time, there is a point in which the priest was praying silently, followed by an elaborate organ solo which Haydn probably intended to play himself. This has given the work its title in German-speaking countries 'Die kleine Orgel-solomesse', the 'little organ solo Mass'.

By this time, Prince Nicolaus had relaxed some of the restrictions on Haydn's work. In 1768, the composer had been allowed to write a cantata, *Applausus*, to celebrate the birthday of the abbot of the beautiful Gothic monastery of Zwettl in lower Austria. Before long, Haydn was allowed to compose works for other patrons and to send copies of his works to a number of noblemen and monasteries. Of course, it was good for the Prince's prestige to have a *Capellmeister* who was so well known, but it was at least equally good for Haydn to make money above his salary by selling his works.

VI

Haydn in the Opera House

The theatre at Eszterháza was opened in 1768 with the first performance of Haydn's *Lo speziale* ('The Apothecary'), a gay, inventive and tuneful work, and gradually during the 1770s the Prince grew more and more interested in opera. He came to prefer Italian comic opera above every other kind except that of his own *Capellmeister*. The operatic season at Eszterháza soon grew to fantastic proportions. For example, during the season of 1786 there were 125 performances, in which seventeen operas were put on the stage; eight of them were produced for the first time. Haydn was required not only to choose and find the music of suitable works. He had to supervise the copying of the parts, the individual coaching of the singers, and also to conduct all the performances himself. He even found time to undertake large-scale revisions of some of the Italian operas he conducted, shortening, substituting arias of his own composition for those he considered poor, re-orchestrating the thin sound of the instruments in many Italian operas of that period and generally re-shaping the music in accordance with his more severe and more logical taste. It remains something of a mystery how Haydn could compose anything at all, but just in this particularly heavy season of 1786, he managed to compose some of his most beautiful symphonies for Paris (Nos. 82, 84, 86) and also six exquisite *concerti* for the King of Naples.

Most of Haydn's operas were composed for special events at the Eszterháza court, like the marriages of the Prince's niece, Countess Lambert, in 1770, which resulted in *Le pescatrici* (The Fisher Women') and of his second son, who later became Nicolaus II, in 1777, which was celebrated by *Il mondo della luna* ('The world on the moon'). For the visit of the Archduke Ferdinand and his wife, in 1775, came *L'incontro improvviso* ('The unexpected meeting'), and the Prince's name-day, in 1779, was marked by the production of *L'isola disabitata* ('The desert island'). Naturally, if these

Prince Nicolaus Esterházy, *c.* 1770

Joseph Haydn, *c.* 1785

works pleased the Prince, they were repeated after their first performance and revived in later years.

In 1776, because his oratorio *Il ritorno di Tobia* ('The return of Tobias') had been a great success when Haydn had conducted it in Vienna a year before, he was commissioned to write an opera for the Emperor's court theatre there. *La vera constanza* ('True constancy') was composed, apparently, in 1776 but the Italian singers and musicians employed in the Vienna opera sabotaged the work, and though Haydn appealed to the Emperor Joseph II, the Emperor could not overcome their resistance to its production, so that Haydn withdrew it and it was first heard at Eszterháza in 1779.

Not even the destruction by fire of his opera house in 1779 could weaken the Prince's appetite for opera, so that *L'isola disabitata* was produced in the marionette theatre, the stage of which had to be enlarged for the occasion. The fire at the opera house had destroyed all its collection of music, including the performance material of the operas Haydn had written up to that date; fortunately, he kept the complete autograph scores in his own apartments so that the music has not been lost. The theatre was rebuilt by 1781, and made even more magnificent than it had originally been.

Haydn wrote three further operas for Eszterháza after the fire—*La fedeltà premiata*, the first to be seen in the rebuilt theatre, *Orlando Paladino* in 1782, and *Armida* in 1784. Like everything he composed his operas show him coming to a close understanding of the problems involved and then setting out to solve them logically and intellectually but without sacrificing emotion to intelligence. The satirical world of *Il mondo della luna*, which takes place on the moon, like a twentieth-century science-fiction work, is not cold but warmly human. We realize how deeply thoughtful a musician Haydn was, but we see that however strong and logical he intended his work to be, it is always expressive as well. He never allowed the form and its conventions to dominate him. *L'infedeltà delusa* ('Inconstancy deluded') composed in 1773, sets a very unconventional story about noble, heroic peasants and a wicked nobleman. The Empress Maria Theresa was present as Prince Nicolaus's guest at its second performance, and at the end she said, 'If I want to hear a good opera, I go to Eszterháza.' *L'isola disabitata* is *opera seria*, in Haydn's day still the most rigidly conventional form of music, but Haydn overrode its conventions. The usual method was to set the dialogue which moves the story onwards to *recitativo secco* ('dry recitative'), in which a voice hurries the words along most of the time on a single note, which it leaves only to translate the inflections of a speaking voice into music; *secco* recitative was accompanied only by punctuating chords here and there, played by a piano or harpsichord. In *L'isola disabitata* Haydn chose to write all the recitatives as *recitativo accompagnato* ('accompanied recitative'), giving them the colour, richness and expressiveness of an orchestral accompaniment.

But his greatest operatic achievements came in his treatment of ensembles and finales. In an ensemble a number of characters express their individual responses to the situation in the story; Haydn gave each of them the power to do so in music characteristic of himself (or herself) while at the same time taking his place as part of a beautifully designed musical piece. He set out to make finales, which customarily end in ensembles, into musical as well as dramatic climaxes; he took into them long passages of the opera text before the final ensemble so that he could design them as extended movements which follow some form that provides them with a musical climax at the appropriate moment, so that we find him writing a finale as a rondo, an instrumental form which he applies to the words and characters to make the right musical effect. In making opera more dramatic, he made it more musical.

When he was asked to compose an opera for the theatre in Prague, Haydn refused on the grounds that his operas were designed for the special conditions of Eszterháza and the musicians whom he knew and had trained there; they could not, he said, make their proper effect elsewhere, and his letter goes on to suggest that the Prague opera director should commission an opera from Mozart, instead. But though Haydn wrote for special singers in a special place on special occasions, we are learning in our days to value his operas properly after nearly two hundred years of neglect. In the age of astronauts, *Il mondo della luna* has become so topical that it has been produced all over Europe, and we are beginning to give proper attention to Haydn's other works for the stage.

By the year 1780 Haydn's orchestra consisted of some twenty-four players (one flute, two oboes, two bassoons, two horns, with optional trumpets and kettledrums, and strings). There were generally a dozen Italian singers, and enough musical personnel among the castle inhabitants to enable Haydn to put together a chorus of his German marionette operas. In the large theatre were given Italian operas and German plays, the latter performed by groups of strolling players who were generally engaged by the Prince to take up residence at Eszterháza for several months of the year; the most famous of these was the Karl Wahl Troupe, who brought Shakespeare to Eszterháza, often in translations which were specially commissioned by

Prince Nicolaus; at the marionette theatre, which was organized and for some years led by the well-known playwright Karl Joseph von Pauersbach, the puppet operas were always given in the German language. In all this rather fantastic display, Haydn himself actually managed to keep a marionette troupe of his own, which must have had very high standards indeed. It is entirely possible that his newly discovered marionette opera *Das abgebrannte Haus* (*Die Feuersbrunst*) ('The house that was burned down, *or* The Conflagration') was composed and performed for Haydn's own private puppet theatre. At any rate Prince Nicolaus seems to have set high store by it, for we find him writing to his Economic Administrator as follows: 'It is known to me that *Capellmeister* Haydn has a small marionette theatre which he displayed with the musicians at *Carneval* last year. I should like to produce something of this kind at Eisenstadt Castle on the 20th, the eve of my wife's birthday. Therefore the whole thing ought to be arranged with Haydn, but in such a way that the Princess doesn't realize anything of the plans . . . Vienna, 13 March 1775, Nicolaus Prince Esterházy.'

The marionette theatre, however, had occupied Haydn before this. On the second day of Maria Theresa's visit in 1773, she saw the first performance of two of his marionette operas—*Der Götterrath* ('The council of the Gods') and *Philemon und Baucis*. The first of the works has been lost, but the music of *Philemon und Baucis* was discovered some years ago; it contains long

Title page for libretto
of *Philemon und Baucis*

arias, large-scale ensembles and even choruses, and is as musically ambitious and expressive as Haydn's operas for human actors.

Haydn also wrote incidental music for some of the plays which were given at the castle: one such piece of music has survived because Haydn later turned it into a symphony (No. 60). The work was originally music for *Der Zerstreute*, a German translation of *Le Distrait* by Jean François Regnard (1655–1709). It was first performed at Eszterháza in the summer of 1774 and later given its first public performance by the Karl Wahl Troupe at Pressburg (who had produced it at Eszterháza), on 22nd November 1774, at which performance one movement (which is now the Finale) had to be repeated. The title of the play could be translated as 'The absent-minded man', and the finale is full of startling examples of musical absent-mindedness; the instruments suddenly break off what they are doing and start something new. The music of its last movement has hardly got under way before the violinists discover that they have tuned their lower strings a semitone too low, and the music has to be stopped until they have retuned.

VII

Growing Fame

The Prince's demands for opera left Haydn with little time and apparently little energy for other compositions. As well as the operas and the church music, he still had to plan, rehearse and perform two concerts every week, and these required new music. He therefore continued to write symphonies, but most of those composed between about 1775 and 1785 are far less adventurous than those he had composed since he first entered the Esterházy service. Several of them, like *L'Imperiale* (No. 53), *The Schoolmaster* (No. 55), and *La Roxelane* (No. 63), are delightful works, skilful, inventive and refined, but one or two are as near to being dull as Haydn's music could become. They are all relaxed and easy-going, but this is not surprising when we consider the amount of work that Haydn had to do to keep up to the court schedule of performances.

For all that, he returned to string quartet writing in 1781. The nine years in which he had written no quartets had occupied his intellect; what he had learned in settling down to solve operatic problems had enriched his technique and left him with new ideas that could be worked out in other forms, so that all his music benefited from his concentration on music for the theatre. The quartets of 1781 were published as Op. 33, and again there is a set of six. They were written, Haydn said, 'in a new and very special way'. By this he meant not only that they used his technique of marrying the symphonic development of themes to counterpoint but also that they achieved his aim of writing quartets in which the four instruments are complete partners, each of them depending on the other three and each doing nothing that is not completely essential to the effect of the work as a whole.

The following year, 1782, saw the composition of the last Mass Haydn was to write before he returned from England in 1795; this was the *Missa cellansis*, known in German as the 'Mariazeller Messe', written for the famous pilgrimage church at Mariazell in Styria. In this justly famous and

53

Finale of String Quartet in G, Op. 33, No. 5,
arranged by Haydn for piano

popular work, Haydn brilliantly combines simple, folk-like tunes appropriate in a work to be sung before crowds of pilgrims from all walks of life—the soprano melody at the beginning of the quick section in the *Kyrie* is an example—with elaborate contrapuntal movements such as the splendid fugue which concludes the work.

Two of Haydn's most popular concertos were composed in this period, that for piano in D (*c.* 1780?) and that for cello in D of 1783. We do not know for what occasion Haydn wrote his last keyboard concerto, but it is a beautiful work with a poetic slow movement and a Hungarian finale. The cello concerto in D was written for the principal cellist in the Esterházy orchestra; Anton Kraft, it is a technically difficult but musically somewhat uneventful piece. The finest concertos of this period are the delicate and lovely works composed in 1786 for the King of Naples, a player of the lyra organizzata, a type of hurdy gurdy the quiet tone of which led Haydn to write the orchestral accompaniment with the greatest delicacy and refinement.

Haydn was now selling his music directly to the publishers. Previously almost everything of Haydn's which had been printed was simply 'pirated' and it is very likely that Haydn never even knew of the existence of many French editions of his music. Indeed, the French were so avid for new works by Haydn, that they very often published works by other composers under Haydn's name. Hitherto Haydn's principal source of extra income had been from selling manuscript copies of his music to monasteries and princely houses; but now he was selling it directly to Artaria and Torricella in Vienna, Forster in London and Sieber and Boyer in Paris.

Towards the end of 1784 Haydn applied to become a member of the Freemasons and was accepted by that body at a Vienna lodge on 11th February 1785. To this period also belong the beginnings of his intimate friendship with W. A. Mozart who dedicated his famous six quartets to Haydn in 1785. The dedication of Mozart's 'Haydn' Quartets expresses the twenty-nine-year-old composer's admiration for the composer from whose music he had learned so much. Mozart had no time at all for most of the music composed by the musicians of his period, and the arrogant way in which he spoke of them seems to have made him many influential enemies. But his sincere affection for Haydn and his great admiration for Haydn's music becomes more impressive when we remember how high and unyielding his standards were. It is also well known that Haydn said to Mozart's father, Leopold, that he considered Wolfgang the greatest composer he knew. Indeed, these two geniuses were drawn to each other amidst the enormous number of mediocre and third-rate compositions which were very often equally or more popular than their own more difficult and intellectual works. When Mozart was rehearsing *Così fan tutte* in 1791, he invited only Haydn and Michael Puchberg, also a brother Freemason, to hear the music. Haydn can have had little opportunity of hearing much of Mozart's music before his stay in Vienna in 1785, but one aspect of his greatness is that as a famous composer already in his fifties he was still able to learn from Mozart. His later music uses counterpoint more freely and is richer in sound because in some things he followed Mozart's example.

In 1785 Haydn received a commission from Cadiz in Spain. Some years later Haydn himself wrote as follows about this composition which is entitled *The Seven Words of the Saviour on the Cross*: 'About fifteen years ago I was asked by the Cathedral Chapter of Cadiz to compose instrumental music on the Seven Words of Jesus on the Cross. In those days they used to give an oratorio every year during Lent at the principal church of Cadiz, and the following circumstances contributed not a little to increasing the general mood. The walls, windows and pillars of the church were clothed in black material, and only one light, hanging in the middle of the church, increased the holy gloom. At noon all the doors to the church were shut; then the music began. Following an appropriate prelude, the bishop ascended the pulpit, said one of the words and then added his own sermon on it. When he had finished, he descended and knelt before the altar. This interval was filled with music. The bishop ascended and descended the pulpit for the second time, third time, and so forth, and each time the orchestra filled in the intervening period with music. This description served me in composing my music. The task of writing seven adagios, of which each should last some ten minutes, to follow one another without tiring the listeners, was not one of the easiest; and I soon found that I could not adhere to the given time. The music was originally without text, and as such it was printed. . . .'

The Seven Words was originally written as an orchestral work scored for strings, two flutes, two oboes, two bassoons, two trumpets, four horns and drums. Two years later, in 1787, Haydn rearranged it as a series of pieces for string quartet, in which form it is frequently heard nowadays though the full orchestral version is not often played. Round about 1794, a certain Frieberth arranged it as a choral work; Haydn apparently disliked what Frieberth had done and in about 1796 made his own choral version, adding two clarinets and two trombones to the orchestra. Baron von Swieten, who was to provide him with words for *The Creation* and *The Seasons*, re-wrote the text that Frieberth had used.

An equally interesting commission came at this time from Paris and re-sulted in the six famous 'Paris symphonies' (Nos. 82 to 87) of 1785 and 1786, which were first performed to enthusiastic audiences at the Parisian Masonic lodge 'Olympique'; this was Haydn's great musical contribution to Freemasonry. All of the other symphonies that Haydn wrote before his visit to London were also destined for Paris.

In 1789 Haydn struck up a firm friendship with Maria Anna von Gen-zinger, whose husband was one of Prince Nicolaus's house doctors. As a result of this friendship we gain an interesting insight into life at Eszterháza during this period from the letters Haydn wrote to her, and the corre-spondence continued during his visit to London.

It seems to have begun when Frau von Genzinger had sent him a copy of a piano arrangement 'of the beautiful Andante of your so admirable composition'. Which Andante she transcribed is not known; apparently it came from a string quartet, and in his reply, and once or twice in later letters, Haydn refers to it as an Adagio. Maria Anna pointed out that, 'I made this arrangement myself, from the score, without the least help from my teacher.' Haydn was delighted both by his new correspondent's obvious affection for his work and by the prospect of friendly correspondence with a cultured, educated woman. To us, the letters always seem to remain very formal: the composer addresses Frau von Genzinger as 'Nobly born, gracious lady' or, in more relaxed moments, as 'Nobly born, most respected and kindest Frau von Genzinger', and in the course of the letters he refers to her always as 'Your Grace'. But after a short time he is sending affectionate messages to her children, referring to them by their nicknames, and gossiping with her about his life in the most free and easy way.

After his New Year stay in Vienna in 1789, he comically described his sorrowful return to Eszterháza in a letter he wrote to her on 9th February:

Well, here I sit in my wilderness—forsaken—like a poor waif—almost without any human society—melancholy—full of memories of past glorious days. . . . I found everything at home in confusion, and for three days I didn't know if was *Capell*-master or *Capell*-servant. Nothing could console me, my whole house was in confusion, my pianoforte, which I usually love so much, was perverse and disobedient, it irritated rather than calmed me, I could sleep only very little, even my dreams persecuted me; and then, just when I was dreaming that I was listening to the opera *The Marriage of Figaro*, that horrible North wind woke me and almost blew my nightcap off my head: I lost 20 lbs weight in three days, for the good Viennese food I had in me disappeared on the journey; alas! alas! I thought to myself as I was eating in the mess here, instead of that delicious slice of beef, a chunk of a cow 50 years old; instead of a ragout with little dumplings, an old sheep with carrots; instead of a Bohemian pheasant, a leathery joint; instead of those fine and delicate oranges, a *Dschabl* or so-called *gross Sallat*; instead of pastry, dry apple-fritters and hazelnuts—and that's what I have to eat. Alas! alas! I thought to myself, if I could only have a little bit of what I couldn't eat up in Vienna. Here is Eszterháza—no one asks me: Would you like some chocolate, with milk or without? Will you take some coffee, black or with cream? What may I offer you, my dear Haydn? Would you like a vanilla or a pineapple ice? If I only had a good piece of Parmesan cheese, especially in

Lent, so that I could more easily swallow those black dumplings and noodles; only today I told our porter here to send me a couple of pounds.

Haydn's head was full of *The Marriage of Figaro* not only because he had just seen Mozart's great opera when it had been revived in Vienna but because he himself was preparing a production for the theatre at Eszterháza. It seems a pity to us that he did not write about his plans for the work when he was trying to amuse Frau von Genzinger with his account of the miseries of life in his 'wilderness'. To her, however, he dedicated his great E flat Piano Sonata, composed in 1790. A year before, the publishing firm of Breitkopf and Härtel, in Leipzig, had asked Haydn for a piano sonata and

Piece for a musical clock, arranged by Haydn from his String Quartet,
Op. 54, No. 2

he had sent them a sonata in C major, no less attractive than the one written for Maria Anna. Like the string quartets which Haydn had written during the 1780s (Opp. 50, 54, and 55), the two sonatas had benefited from all the music he had written up to that time and all the musical problems he had been set to solve. They are intimate works, meant for their player and, perhaps, a few friends but not addressed to the general public. They are thoughtful, and are worked out with remarkable intellectual mastery, but their thought goes in step with a great range of emotion, for Haydn the master of musical form was always a composer who wrote because he had something to express.

Haydn's manuscript of the Sonata in E flat major

In 1790 Haydn received another commission for the King of Naples: a series of *notturni* which he composed in the summery stillness of the last season that he was to know at Eszterháza. Mozart's *The Marriage of Figaro* had three performances in August and September 1790, but on 28th September Nicolaus died. Perhaps for this occasion, Haydn composed his severe and beautiful *Libera me*, which was discovered in 1966 in the parish church at Eisenstadt.

Prince Anton, who succeeded to the Esterházy title, was not interested in music. He discharged all his musicians except those he needed for his chapel services and paid Haydn a salary of 400 florins to keep him officially in Esterházy employment though he was left with no *Capellmeister*'s work to do and free to go wherever he wanted and to do whatever he chose. Prince Nicolaus had left Haydn an annual pension of 1,000 florins. The salary and the pension would continue whatever Haydn did, and he was quickly offered several valuable posts, including one from his admirer and patron the King of Naples. While he was thinking of his future and undecided which position to accept, the opportunity of real freedom came to him for the first time.

Immediately after the Prince's death, Haydn went to Vienna, where one morning a stranger knocked on his door and introduced himself as Johann Peter Salomon, the Bonn-born impresario who had a spectacular career in London as a violinist, conductor and concert promoter. He had come to take Haydn to England, and since the new Prince Esterházy, Anton, no longer required Haydn's active services as *Capellmeister*, the composer decided to go. Mozart said to him 'but you don't know the language', to which Haydn answered, 'My language is understood all over the world.' At a farewell luncheon both Haydn and Mozart wept and Mozart was suddenly filled with a dread premonition, 'We shall not see each other ever again.' On 15th December 1790 Haydn and Salomon set off for England; it was the greatest adventure of Haydn's life.

The Esterházy coat of arms, another
watermark in paper used
by Haydn

VIII

London 1791–92

Haydn often said that his years in England were the happiest of his life; indeed, he had every reason to think so. When he left Esterházy's service in 1790, he had hardly two thousand gulden to his name in savings as the tangible result of nearly thirty years' exhausting and unremitting work. His financial situation was, all things considered, not all that much better than Mozart's, who found it impossible to live on his income, though Haydn was a better businessman and his prospects (with London) were perhaps rosier. He had, moreover, a good pension to fall back on, which Mozart had not. But it was certainly England that made Haydn independently wealthy and set the seal on his international fame, for it is mostly the so-called 'Salomon' or 'London' symphonies which have carried Haydn's name all over the world ever since.

Haydn arrived in London early in January 1791. He wrote his first impressions of the largest city in the world to his friend Maria Anna von Genzinger in a letter of 8th January:

Nobly born,
Gracious Lady!
I hope that you will have received my last letter from Calais. I should have written you immediately after my arrival in London, but I wanted to wait a few days so as to be able to write about several things at once. So I can tell you that on the 1st inst., New Year's Day, after attending early mass, I boarded the ship at 7.30 a.m. and at 5 in the afternoon I arrived, thank God! safe and sound in Dower [that was how he spelled Dover]. At the beginning, for the first 4 whole hours, we had almost no wind, and the ship went so slowly that in these 4 hours we didn't go further than one single English mile, and there are 24 between Calais and Dower. Our ship's captain, in an evil temper, said that if the wind did not change, we should have to spend the whole night at sea. Fortunately,

however, towards 11.30 o'clock a wind arose and blew so favourably that by 4 o'clock we covered 22 miles. Since the tide, which had just begun to ebb, prevented our large vessel from reaching the pier, 2 smaller ships came out to meet us as we were still fairly far out at sea, and into these we and our luggage were transferred, and thus at last, though exposed to a medium gale, we landed safely. The large vessel stood out to sea five hours longer, till the tide turned and it could finally dock. Some of the passengers were afraid to board the little boats and stayed on board, but I followed the example of the greater number. I remained on deck during the whole passage, so as to gaze my fill at that mighty monster, the ocean. [In all his fifty-eight years, Haydn had never before seen the sea.] So long as it was calm, I wasn't afraid at all, but towards the end, when the wind grew stronger and stronger, and I saw the monstrous high waves rushing at us, I became a little frightened, and a little indisposed, too. But I overcame it all and arrived safely, without (forgive me) vomiting, on shore. Most of the passengers were ill, and looked like ghosts, but since I went on to London, I didn't feel the effects of the journey right away; but then I needed 2 days to recover. Now, however, I am fresh and well again, and occupied in looking at this endlessly huge city of London, whose various beauties and marvels quite astonished me. I immediately paid the necessary calls, such as to the Neapolitan Ambassador and to our own; both called on me in return 2 days later, and 4 days ago I lunched with the former—N.B. at 6 o'clock in the evening, as is the custom here.

My arrival caused a great sensation throughout the whole city, and I went the round of all the newspapers for 3 successive days. Everyone wants to know me. I had to dine out 6 times up to now, and if I wanted, I could dine out every day; but first I must consider my health, and second my work. Except for the nobility, I admit no callers till 2 o'clock in the afternoon, and at 4 o'clock I dine at home with Mon. Salomon. I have nice and comfortable, but expensive, lodgings. My landlord is Italian, and also a cook, and serves me 4 very respectable meals; we each pay 1 fl. 30 kr. a day excluding wine and beer, but everything is terribly expensive here. Yesterday I was invited to a grand amateur concert, but I arrived a bit late, and when I showed my ticket they wouldn't let me in but led me to an antechamber, where I had to wait till the piece which was then being played in the hall was over. Then they opened the door, and I was conducted, on the arm of the entrepreneur, up the centre of the hall to the front of the orchestra, amid universal applause, and there I was stared at and greeted by a great number of English compliments. I

Above, an incomplete oil portrait of Mozart by Joseph Lange, *c.* 1790; *above right*, Joseph Haydn, a silhouette by Hieronymous Löschenkhl, 1785; *right*, an engraving by Johann Heinrich Lipps of Beethoven, 1801

The Creation, the frontispiece for the vocal
score of the Pleyel edition, 1801

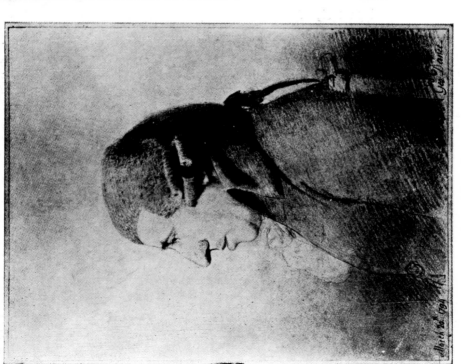

A pencil drawing of Haydn in 1794
by George Dance

was assured that such honours had not been conferred on anyone for 50 years. After the concert I was taken to a handsome adjoining room, where a table for 200 persons, with many places set, was prepared for all the amateurs; I was supposed to be seated at the head of the table, but since I had dined out on that day and had eaten more than usual, I declined this honour, with the excuse that I was not feeling very well, but despite this I had to drink the harmonious health, in Burgundy, of all the gentlemen present; they all returned the toast, and then allowed me to be taken home. All this, my gracious lady, was very flattering to me, and yet I wished I could fly for a time to Vienna, to have more quiet in which to work, for the noise that the common people make as they sell their wares in the street is intolerable. At present I am working on symphonies, because the libretto of the opera is not yet decided on, but in order to have more quiet I shall have to rent a room far from the centre of town. I would gladly write you in more detail, but I am afraid of missing the mail-coach. Meanwhile I am, with kindest regards to your husband, Fräulein Pepi and all the others, most respectfully,

Your Grace's

most sincere and obedient servant,
Joseph Haydn.

The new opera was *L'anima del filosofo* ('The Philosopher's Soul'), with the subtitle *Orfeo ad Euridice*. Because of rivalry between the two London opera houses—the King, George III, supported one, and the Prince of Wales, later George IV, the other—Haydn's last and in many respects most adventurous opera was never to our knowledge performed in his lifetime. The first performance we know of took place in Florence in 1951. Haydn worked into this last opera all his thoughts about music for the stage which he had not been able to express in his previous works for the Esterházy theatre. He had a large and well-trained chorus, and the orchestra was also the largest Haydn ever used for opera and includes flutes, oboes, two *cors anglais* (instruments which were unknown in London at that time), clarinets, bassoons, horns, trumpets, trombones, timpani, harpsichord, harp and strings.

For this first season of Salomon's concerts he composed two new symphonies, Nos. 95 and 96. The subscription concerts that Salomon organized included not only Haydn, who 'presided at the pianoforte', but also the leading singers of the day. Normally, concerts in Haydn's period were conducted by the first violinist, who played as he stood facing the orchestra.

E

This was the way in which Haydn conducted at Eszterháza, and it explains why in England the first violinist is called the 'leader'; his title in other countries is 'concert master'. A piano concerto, however, would be conducted by its soloist, who could beat time when he was not playing, and control the performance while his hands were occupied probably by a few movements of his head. Haydn sat at the piano for his London concerts because he could not take the place of Salomon, who promoted them, playing a piano part which simply reinforced the essential harmonies. Haydn had brought with him a trunk full of compositions unknown in England: arias, string quartets (those of Op. 64 written in 1790), the *notturni* for the King of Naples of 1790 which he re-wrote for London, and other useful works.

The first concert took place on 11th March 1791. The programme was as follows:

HANOVER-SQUARE. MR. SALOMON respectfully acquaints the Nobility and Gentry, that his CONCERTS will open without further delay on Friday next, the 11th of March, and continue every succeeding Friday.

PART I

Overture—Rosetti
Song—Sig(nor) Tajana.
Concerto Oboe—Mr. Harrington.
Song—Signora Storace.
Concerto Violin—Madame Gautherot.
Recitativo and Aria—Signor David (Composed by Rusi).

PART II

New Grand Overture—Haydn.
Recitative and Aria—Signora Storace.
Concertante, Pedal Harp and Pianoforte—Madame
Krumpholtz and Mr. Dusseck (Dussek).
Composed by Mr. Dusseck.
Rondo—Signor David (Composed by Andreozzi).
Full Piece—Kozeluck (Koželuh).
Mr. HAYDN will be at the Harpsichord.
Leader of the Band, Mr. SALOMON.
Tickets transferable, as usual, Ladies to Ladies and
Gentlemen to Gentlemen only.

The Ladies' tickets are Green, the Gentlemen's Black. The Subscribers are entreated to give particular orders to their Coachmen to set down and take up at the Side Door in the Street, with the Horses' Heads towards the Square.

The Door in the Square is for Chairs only.

The Press was enthusiastic and we read in the *Diary* as follows:

HANOVER SQUARE

The long delayed Concert, undertaken this year by Mr. SALOMON, took place last night, and was attended by a numerous and very elegant audience. A musical treat, under the immediate direction of the great HAYDN, promised the connoisseurs an exquisite repast, and they were not disappointed. . . . A new grand overture by HAYDN, was received with the highest applause, and universally deemed a composition as pleasing as scientific. The audience was so enraptured, that by unanimous desire, the second movement was encored, and the third was vehemently demanded a second time also, but the modesty of the Composer prevailed too strongly to admit a repetition. . . .

We also have an interesting description of Haydn's new arrangement of the orchestra from the diary of Mrs. Papendiek, one of the Ladies-in-Waiting to the Queen:

. . . The wished-for night at length arrived, and as I was anxious to be near the performers I went early. Mr. Papendiek followed from the Queen's House, and I got an excellent seat on a sofa at the right-hand side. The orchestra was arranged on a new plan. The pianoforte was in the centre, at each extreme end the double basses, then on each side two violoncellos, then two tenors or violas and two violins, and in the hollow of the piano a desk on a high platform for Salomon with his ripieno. At the back, verging down to a point at each end, all these instruments were doubled, giving the requisite number for a full orchestra. Still further back, raised high up, were the drums, and on either side the trumpets, trombones, bassoons, oboes, clarinets, flutes &c., in numbers according to the requirements of the symphonies and other music to be played on the different evenings.

. . . The second act invariably opened with a new symphony composed for the night. Haydn of course conducted his own music, and generally that of other composers, in fact all through the evening.

The Hanover Square Rooms are calculated to hold 800 persons exclusive of the performers. By the beginning of the second act we concluded that all had arrived who intended to come, and though we knew that Salomon's subscription list was not full, we had hoped for additions during the evening. But no; and I regret to make this observation of my countrymen, that until they know what value they are likely to receive for their money they are slow in coming forward with it. . . .

Now the anxious moment arrived, and Salomon having called 'attention' with his bow, the company rose to a person and stood through the whole of the first movement.

The effect was imposingly magnificent. The instruments might all be said to have an obbligato part, so perfectly was the whole combination conceived and carried out. . . . Salomon was wound up to a pitch of enthusiasm beyond himself. The applause was great. The public was satisfied, and Haydn was very properly taken up.

The rival concert organization, known as the Professional Concerts, had seen the danger that a celebrity like Haydn might easily win the entire London audience if he were not strenuously opposed. Therefore in December 1791 they brought to London a European celebrity of their own for the 1792 season, Ignaz Joseph Pleyel, who was thirty-four years old and had studied with Haydn in the 1770s; Pleyel had a great affection and admiration for his old teacher and probably did not know that he had been invited to London to lead a campaign against Haydn. The Professional Concerts announced that Haydn was an old man, that he could not possibly produce all the works which he had undertaken to compose and perform in London, that his style was out of date and that Pleyel would prove to be his superior.

Haydn naturally attended Pleyel's first concert and applauded enthusiastically. Pleyel, too, refused to be Haydn's enemy and the two met as old friends. When Haydn's first concert was given the difference between a supreme genius and a good, honest composer was only too clear. There was no more attempt at opposition.

Like many of Haydn's symphonies, the twelve 'London' or 'Salomon' Symphonies, which seem in their brilliance of style and their rich expressiveness to sum up everything he had to say in symphonic form, have been incorrectly numbered. They are Nos. 93 to 104. The work played at Haydn's first concert was No. 92 which he had composed in 1789 but was not yet known in England. For a later concert in the 1791 season, he wrote No. 96 which has come to be known as the 'Miracle' Symphony. In some mysterious way it has been connected with an incident which occurred almost three years later at the concert when No. 102 had its first performance. The chandelier over the centre of the hall crashed down from the ceiling into the auditorium, and the 'miracle' was that no one was injured, because, the story goes, everybody had crowded to the front of the hall to cheer Haydn as he walked on to the platform. Nobody knows how No. 96 came to be coupled with this incident.

But, like newspaper critics and Mrs. Papendiek, the audience at the first concert was wildly enthusiastic. Dr. Burney wrote that Haydn had an 'electrifying effect upon all present', and after a single concert he became a popular favourite; the newspapers began to hope that he would settle permanently in England. He was soon received by the Prince of Wales and became a favourite of London society.

At the end of May a great Handel festival was given in Westminster Abbey with an enormous chorus and orchestra of one thousand persons. Haydn attended and was much moved during the 'Hallelujah' chorus in *Messiah*, where it is reported that 'he wept like a child', crying out: 'Here is the master of us all!'

The composer was easily persuaded to stay in London for another season. In July Oxford University conferred upon Haydn the title of Doctor of Music.

As his 'exercise' to obtain the degree when it was offered to him, he sent the university a very complex 'canon cancrizans' for three voices. The simplest form of canon is a round like 'London's burning', but the word 'cancrizans' means that Haydn's Oxford Canon can be sung backwards by three voices each entering in turn while it is being sung forwards in the same way. Its words are simply 'Thy voice, O Harmony, is divine', and he used the same music again a few years later for the words of the First Commandment when he made a series of canons as music for the Ten Commandments. At the second of the three concerts which he gave in Oxford, his Ninety-Second Symphony was played for the first time in Oxford. It had been the most popular work of the 1791 season in London, but English audiences have always known it as the 'Oxford Symphony'.

At the final concert, Haydn wore his doctor's gown of cherry and cream coloured silk, and this stimulated the audience to even louder applause than he had grown used to in England, so he grasped the lapels of the gown, holding them out towards the audience and calling out to his admirers, 'I thank you.' Some of them replied, 'You speak very good English!'

All the same, Haydn felt self-conscious in his splendid academic robe; it

Canone cancrizans a tre

made him feel foolish, and in his current Notebook he made a note of the costs involved in becoming a Doctor of Music:

'I had to pay 1½ guineas for having the bells rung at Oxforth in connection with my doctor's degree, and ½ guinea for [the hire of] the robe. The trip cost six guineas.'

For all that, he was flattered by the honour he had received and often used the title 'Doctor of Music' in writing formal letters. When, after his return to Austria, Prince Nicolaus II addressed him in the third person —the way in which Austrian noblemen would normally address someone beneath their notice—Haydn pointed out that he was a Doctor of Music at the University of Oxford, and should not be spoken to as 'he' and 'him'.

In the summer, he visited his new English friends in the country, and his curiosity about this new land and its inhabitants are vividly reflected in the Notebooks he kept and in his letters to Vienna. The Notebooks remind us that Haydn was an extremely intelligent, quick-thinking man, thoughtful and observant, who suddenly, in his late fifties, was provided with new sights, new experiences and new interests. He made notes of whatever seemed unusual, quaint, or peculiar—London prices, English habits and customs, stories that amused him and notes about people he met, the music he heard, and the halls or theatres in which he heard it:

'The national debt of England is estimated to be over two hundred millions. Recently it was calculated that if they had to make up a convoy to pay this sum in silver, the waggons, end on end, would reach from London to Yorck, that is, 200 miles, presuming that each could not carry more than £6000.'

He was taken to Ascot to watch the races, and his note carefully describes the course, the prices of places in the stands, the jockeys' dress, the horses and their value, gamblers and the sideshows. A witty reply to a heckler by the politician Charles James Fox is noted down. Sometimes, he gets English customs confused; 'On 5th November,' he wrote, 'the boys celebrate the day on which the Guys set the town on fire.'

In November 1791, he stayed with the Prince of Wales (the Prince Regent who became George IV) and his brother the Duke of York, at the Duke's country house at Oaklands, in Surrey. This was something to remember for a man who had spent the better part of his life wearing court livery and treated with the friendly consideration men give to their good servants. The Duchess of York, who was the daughter of the King of Prussia and only seventeen, charmed him. Haydn told Maria Anna Genzinger, 'She treated me most graciously and said many flattering things. . . . On the second day she remained at my side from 10 o'clock in the evening, when the music began, to 2 o'clock in the morning. Nothing but Haydn was played. I conducted the symphonies from the pianoforte and the sweet little thing sat beside me on my left and hummed all the pieces from memory. . . . The Prince of Wales sat on my right side and played with us on his violoncello, very tolerably.'

Often he was invited to civic banquets, and at some he was guest of honour. All his life he had been at the beck and call of princes, conscious of the gap between a musician and a nobleman, but he felt in England as if the work he had done had ennobled him. Perfect strangers walked up to him in the street and said, 'You are a great man.' His letter to Frau von Genzinger continues:

> . . . I have been residing in the country, amid lovely scenery, with a banker, whose heart and family resemble the Genzingers, and where I live as in a monastery. God be praised! I am in good health, with the exception of my usual rheumatic state. I work hard, and in the early mornings, when I walk in the wood alone with my English grammar, I think of my Creator, of my family, and of all the friends I have left—and of these you are the most valued of all. . . . Oh, my dear good lady, how sweet is some degree of liberty! I had a good Prince, but was obliged at times to be dependent on base souls. I often sighed for release, and now I have it in some measure. I am quite sensible of this benefit, though my mind is burdened with more work. The consciousness of being no longer a bond-servant sweetens all my toils. But, dear as my liberty is to me, I do hope on my return again to enter the service of Prince Esterházy, solely for the sake of my family. . . . You shall receive my promised new symphony two months hence; but in order to inspire me with good ideas, I beg you to write to me, and a long letter too. . . .

The closest of all his London friends was Rebecca Schroeter, a well-born, highly educated widow whose husband had been music teacher to the Queen until his death in 1788. Mrs. Schroeter took piano lessons from Haydn, and wrote often to him between their meetings. She obviously fell in love with the humorous, gently good-natured great man; her first letter to him is a very formal note explaining when she will be at home so that he can call to give her a lesson, but very soon the letters begin 'My Dear' or even 'My Dearest'. To make her even more attractive to a musician, she loved and understood Haydn's music as deeply as she loved its composer, and it seems that he became as fond of her as she was of him. If he replied to any of her letters, his answers have been lost, but when he returned to London in 1794, he took lodgings near her house. In his old age, he showed a friend a packet of letters. 'Those are from an English lady who fell in love with me,' he said. 'She was a very attractive woman, and still handsome though over sixty; and had I been free I should certainly have married her.'

Probably Haydn was wrong about her age. Her husband had been thirty-eight when he died, so that unless Mrs. Schroeter had been much older than her husband, she must have been in her early forties when Haydn knew her.

At the beginning of 1792, the news of Mozart's death at the age of thirty-five reached London; it shocked Haydn unbearably. His Notebook has only one sentence about it—'Mozart died on 5th Dec. 1791', but a few days later he wrote to his friend and fellow-Freemason, Johann Michael Puchberg, who had been a good friend to Mozart in the poverty that had made the young composer's final years of life miserable:

> ... For some time I was beside myself about his death and could not believe that Providence would so soon claim the life of such an indispensable man. I only regret that before his death he could not convince the English, who are benighted in this respect, of his greatness—a subject about which I have been preaching to them every single day.

In the 1792 season, Haydn conducted his four new symphonies and a new *concertante* for oboe, bassoon, violin, cello and orchestra, as well as a new choral and orchestral work; he called it a 'madrigal', entitled 'The Storm', his first attempt at English words. It was all a triumphant success, and whole movements were repeated. *The Times*, which had barely acknowledged Haydn's existence hitherto, finally broke down its resistance to him with the beginning of this new season. After the first concert on 17th February 1792, it said of Haydn's Symphony No. 93:

SALOMON'S CONCERT

The first Subscription Concert took place last Friday, at Hanover Square. The established musical judges present all agreed that it went off with surprising effect and rigid exactness. No Band in the World can go better.

A new Overture from the pen of the incomparable *Haydn*, formed one considerable branch of this stupendous musical tree.

Such a combination of excellence was contained in every movement, as inspired all the performers as well as the audience with enthusiastic ardour.

Novelty of idea, agreeable caprice, and whim combined with all *Haydn*'s sublime and wanten grandeur, gave additional consequence to the *soul* and feelings of every individual present.

The Critic's eye brightened with additional lustre—then was the moment that the great Painter might have caught—that, which cannot be thrown on the human frame, but on such rare and great occasion. . . .

When Symphony No. 98 was first played on 2nd March 1792, the first *and* last movement were encored: Haydn wrote himself a harpsichord (or possibly pianoforte) solo in this finale which brought the house down. Later someone present wrote: 'The Writer of this Memoire remembers him to have executed [it] with the utmost Accuracy and Precision.' On 3rd May 1792, Haydn gave his benefit concert and one of the extant tickets tells us that, 'Ye Duchess of York was present for the first time in England & 1500 people entered the door.'

About the end of June 1792, Haydn left England and stopped on his return at Bad Godesberg, where the Archbishop-Elector of Cologne's orchestra gave a dinner in his honour, and Beethoven, a young court musician there, submitted a cantata to the elderly composer, who praised it and encouraged the young man to continue his studies, promising to be his teacher if he would go to Vienna. In December 1792, Beethoven came to Vienna to be Haydn's pupil. It appears that Haydn actually intended to take Beethoven with him on his next trip to London. The following now famous letter (it was discovered only before the Second World War in Vienna) reveals a great deal of Haydn's insight as a teacher:

HAYDN TO MAXIMILIAN FRANZ, THE ELECTOR OF COLOGNE, BONN:
Serene Electoral Highness!
I humbly take the liberty of sending Your Serene Electoral Highness some musical works, *viz.*, a Quintet, an eight-part Parthie, an oboe Concerto, Variations for the fortepiano, and a Fugue, compositions of my dear pupil Beethoven, with whose care I have been graciously entrusted. I flatter myself that these pieces, which I may recommend as evidence of his assiduity over and above his actual studies, may be graciously accepted by Your Serene Electoral Highness. Connoisseurs and non-connoisseurs must candidly admit, from these present pieces, that Beethoven will in time fill the position of one of Europe's greatest com-

posers, and I shall be proud to be able to speak of myself as his teacher; I only wish that he might remain with me a little while longer.

While we are on the subject of Beethoven, Your Serene Electoral Highness will perhaps permit me to say a few words concerning his financial status. 100 (ducats) were allotted to him during the past year. Your Serene Electoral Highness is no doubt yourself convinced that this sum was insufficient, and not even enough to live from; undoubtedly Your Highness also had his own reasons for choosing to send him into the great world with such a paltry sum. Under these circumstances, and to prevent him from falling into the hands of usurers, I have in part gone bail for him and in part lent him money myself, with the result that he owes me 500 fl., of which not a Kreutzer was spent unnecessarily; which sum I would ask you to send to him here. And since the interest on borrowed money grows continually, and is very tedious for an artist like Beethoven anyway, I think that if Your Serene Electoral Highness were to send him 1000 fl. for the coming year, Your Highness would earn his eternal gratitude, and at the same time relieve him of all his distress: for the teachers which are absolutely essential for him, and the display which is necessary if he is to gain admission into numerous salons, reduce this sum to such an extent that only the bare minimum remains. As for the extravagance which one fears will tempt any young man who goes into the great world, I think I can answer for that to Your Serene Electoral Highness: for a hundred circumstances have confirmed me in my opinion that he is capable of sacrificing everything quite unconstrainedly for his art. In view of so many tempting occasions, this is most remarkable, and gives every security to Your Serene Electoral Highness—in view of the gracious kindness that we expect—that Your Highness will not be wasting any of your grace on usurers as far as Beethoven is concerned. In the hope that Your Serene Electoral Highness will continue his further patronage of my dear pupil by graciously acceding to this my request, I am, with profound respect,

Your Serene Electoral Highness'
most humble and obedient
Joseph Haydn
Capell Meister von Fürst Nicolaus Esterházy

Vienna, 23rd November 1793.

The Elector, who was paying Beethoven's salary as one of the musicians of the Electoral Court in Bonn during Beethoven's absence in Vienna, and who was treating the 100 ducats as a yearly grant, was not very impressed by Haydn's letter. His reply pointed out that all the compositions Haydn had sent to him except the fugue had been heard in Bonn before Beethoven left there, and he suggested that the young man had better return to his normal duties before he got seriously into debt and other bad habits.

Haydn spent the year at Vienna and Eisenstadt, writing new quartets for London (which later became known as Opps. 71 and 74) and drafting some of the new symphonies. On 26th January 1793, Haydn suffered the loss of one of his greatest friends: Maria Anna von Genzinger, who was only forty-two when she died.

IX

Return to London

In January 1794 Haydn again set off for London, taking with him this time Johann Elssler to act as his copyist and *valet de chambre*.

The second London sojourn produced even more profound and brilliant works than the first. Apart from Haydn's last six symphonies (Nos. 99–104) he also wrote his greatest piano trios, three of which, including that with the famous 'Gipsy Rondo', he dedicated to Mrs. Schroeter, as well as his last and three greatest piano sonatas. The string quartets which he had composed the year before in Vienna (Op. 71) were now performed at Salomon's concerts. These works are different from Haydn's earlier quartets because they are the first compositions of this kind ever written directly for an audience to hear in the concert hall rather than for a group of players to enjoy in a private room. Part of their spirit also derives from the fact that they were written with the special ability of Johann Peter Salomon as a violinist in mind, and Salomon's brilliant tone was no doubt admirably suited for these new works. They might be justly described as symphonic string quartets: they have the same kind of bold and dramatic accents that we find in Haydn's late symphonies.

The Press was also more detailed in its criticism of the new works. We find, for example, the following note about Symphony No. 99 in the *Morning Chronicle* of 19th February 1794:

> . . . But the richest part of the banquet, as usual, was due to the wonderful Haydn.
>
> His new quartetto gave pleasure by its variety, gaiety, and the fascination of its melody and harmony through all its movements: and the overture, being performed with increasing accuracy and effect, was received with increasing rapture. The first movement was encored . . . but indeed the pleasure the whole gave was continual; and the genius of Haydn, astonishing[ly] inexhaustible, and sublime, was the general theme.

The brilliant violin technique of the famous composer G. B. Viotti, who had lived in London since 1792, had a profound effect on the string playing of the London orchestras of this period and is often mentioned by contemporary critics together with their praise of Haydn's genius as a composer. It is no exaggeration to say that Haydn as well as Salomon and Viotti were responsible for the constitution of the modern orchestra as we know it.

The greatest success that Haydn enjoyed in England was undoubtedly the 'Military' Symphony. The *Morning Chronicle* of 9th April 1794 reports:

SALOMON'S NINTH CONCERT
Though under the necessity of repeating the same names (for where are their equals?) and the same praises, which never sufficiently express the delicious sensations that these Performers at some moments excite, yet to be silent would be flagrant injustice. . . . Another new Symphony, by Haydn, was performed for the second time; and the middle movement was again received with absolute shouts of applause. Encore! encore! encore! resounded from every seat: the Ladies themselves could not forbear. It is the advancing to battle; and the march of men, the sounding of the charge, the thundering of the onset, the clash of arms, the groans of the wounded, and what may well be called the hellish roar of war increase to a climax of horrid sublimity! which, if others can conceive, he alone can execute; at least he alone hitherto has effected these wonders.

Haydn was now introduced at Court and George III asked him to stay in England; the Queen offered him a suite in Windsor Castle. Haydn considered the idea carefully, but he was no longer young (in 1795 he was sixty-three) and wanted to live out his old age in peace in his own country: the Napoleonic War, which was steadily increasing in violence, was also threatening to isolate England completely, just as England's naval blockade effectively isolated the Continent.

In 1795 Salomon combined his efforts to produce a new series entitled the Opera Concerts. Viotti was now the leader, but Salomon played with the band and frequently appeared as soloist. The concerts were no longer held in the elegant Hanover Square Rooms but in the King's Theatre. The orchestra, which had consisted of some forty players in the Salomon concerts, was now augumented to sixty, nearly the size of our modern symphony orchestra. Haydn composed his last three symphonies, Nos. 102–104, for the Opera Concerts, and they, too were received with the greatest applause. Of Symphony No. 102 in B flat, which many consider to be Haydn's greatest orchestral work, the *Morning Chronicle* of 17th February 1795 writes: 'What shall we say of HAYDN, and the sublime, the magic Overture [symphony], with which he began the second act [part]? The rapture it gave cannot be communicated by words: to be known it must be heard.'

During this last visit to London, Haydn composed many new works. The following twelve pages are devoted to examples taken from the music he was then writing. Apart from the variety of moods, it clearly shows what a creative period of Haydn's life this was.

Country Dance

Two Marches

2. March

Song 'Trust not too much'

Slow movement from the Piano Trio in E flat major, No. 22

Haydn's last benefit concert took place on 4th May 1795. At it, Brigida Giorgi-Banti sang a new vocal work by Haydn, entitled 'Scena di Berenice'. This large-scale concert aria is one of the greatest vocal pieces of the eighteenth century. At this same concert Haydn conducted some of his most popular symphonies and wrote in his diary: 'The whole company was thoroughly pleased and so was I. I made four thousand gulden on this evening: such a thing is only possible in England.' He told his biographer Griesinger that he took in a total of some twenty-four thousand gulden (more than £2,000) during his English trips, of which about nine thousand were used for the trips, for his stay and for other costs.

Meanwhile, Prince Anton Esterházy had died, and Haydn's new Prince, Nicolaus II, had decided to reconstitute the princely band and choir. He requested Haydn to come home to Vienna and to once more take up his duties as active *Capellmeister*. And so in the middle of August 1795 Haydn sorrowfully took leave of his 'dear English friends' and returned to Vienna rich, famous and the greatest composer of the day. The English never forgot him and continued to cherish his music from that day onwards.

X

Vienna—Eisenstadt 1796—1809

Between his two London trips Haydn had purchased a house in what was then a suburb of Vienna called Gumpendorf. The street was known in Haydn's day as the Untere Steingasse and has now been renamed Haydngasse. The composer submitted a request to the *Magistrat* of the city of Vienna on 14th August 1793 concerning his plan to enlarge the building and when he returned from England this new house was his principal Viennese residence; he also, however, maintained what he called an *Absteigquartier* (literally a 'jumping-off place') in the old city.

Prince Nicolaus II Esterházy abandoned Eszterháza Castle completely and established his summer residence at Eisenstadt. He required of Haydn, apart from administrative duties, only to compose a mass once every year for the name-day of his wife, the Princess Maria Hermenegild, of whom Haydn was particularly fond. Thus we owe to this circumstance Haydn's six last and greatest masses, written between 1796 and 1802.

These are the first masses that Haydn had written since 1782, and they each use four soloists, a choir and, perhaps because the size of the Esterházy band had been reduced in Prince Anton's days, in all except two, a large orchestra. The exceptions are the *Missa in angustiis* ('Mass in time of need'), which is also called the *Nelson Mass* (1798) and the *Theresienmesse*, 1799. The *Nelson Mass* gets its name from a great blaze of trumpets at the end of its *Benedictus* ('Blessed is He that cometh in the Name of the Lord'), an almost frightening stroke of drama in a movement which Haydn usually regarded as a beautifully lyrical slow movement. While Haydn was composing it, Admiral Nelson blew the French fleet out of the water at Aboukir in Egypt, and afterwards this music was always associated with England's greatest naval commander. In 1800 Nelson and Lady Hamilton visited Eisenstadt to meet the composer; Lady Hamilton herself was an accomplished singer, and the great sailor exchanged his gold watch for the great composer's pen. Apart from the three trumpets which convince us that the coming of the

Lord will be glorious but terrifying, the work is scored only for strings, timpani and organ, the latter playing an elaborate solo part. The *Theresienmesse* uses clarinets, trumpets, strings, timpani and organ.

Another of these masses is called *Missa in Tempore Belli* (Mass in time of war'), and the prayer for peace with which it ends ('Lamb of God, that takest away the sins of the world, grant us Thy peace') is accompanied by the trumpets and drums of war, sounds growing all too familiar in the Europe of Haydn's old age, as the armies of revolutionary France first defeated the powers which set out to overthrow the revolution and then, under Napoleon, became aggressors determined to dominate the Continent. All the masses range in mood from great tenderness, in the words of the Creed which speak of the incarnation of Christ, to movements of great lyrical rapture for the *Benedictus* and fiery, inventive fugues at the end of the *Gloria in excelsis* ('Glory be to God on High'), which thinks of the eternal glory of God, and the end of the Creed, a statement of belief in 'the life of the world to come'. The 1796 Mass is known as The Mass of St. Bernard of Offida, or, in Germany, as the *Heiligemesse*, for *Heilig* is the German word for 'Holy', and the melody of a German hymn, 'Holy, holy, holy' is buried in the tenor part of its *Sanctus* ('Holy, holy, holy, Lord God of Sabaoth'); the fifth is called the Creation Mass, for the *Qui tollis* of the *Gloria* uses a theme from Haydn's oratorio *The Creation*, completed in 1798; the sixth, in German-speaking countries, is the *Harmoniemesse* because of the importance of wind instruments in its orchestra, *Harmonie* being the German term for a band of wind instruments. The fact that they have been given such nicknames, apart from the names given to them by their composer, shows how deeply they are loved by the German-speaking countries, in which they have always been as popular as the twelve great 'London' symphonies have always been among English audiences.

In a sense, the six masses are great choral symphonies written to the glory of God; they present and develop their themes in a symphonic way, and are, like symphonies, built up of movements of related but contrasted moods and tempos. The four soloists are not used in long, elaborate arias but as a contrasting tone colour, different from both the orchestra and the choir. Haydn wrote the masses between his sixty-fourth and seventy-first birthdays, but they are as daring, as inventive and as deeply thought out as anything he had ever written; this means, of course, that they are exciting, moving, expressive music. 'I am rather proud of my masses,' said Haydn to his biographer Griesinger. It was natural for him to be so, for they are masterpieces as important as any music he had ever written.

In 1796, Haydn wrote his Trumpet Concerto, the last and most remarkable of his works for solo instrument and orchestra. The standard trumpet of Haydn's time was not able to play a complete scale and therefore was only used to play themes like the signal calls for which it is used in an army or, in forceful passages, to reinforce the harmony. A trumpeter named Weidinger invented an improved trumpet which, through the use of keys, could play all the notes of the chromatic scale (represented on a keyboard instrument by the black keys as well as the white). This made it possible for a trumpeter to play any type of melody and seems to have stimulated Haydn to write his concerto; he was the first composer of any importance to make use of Weidinger's keyed trumpet (which was soon supplanted by trumpets with the modern valve mechanism also applied to horns). The work is expressive, emotional, rich in feeling and shares in the wonderful combination of serenity with gaiety which came to the composer as he grew old.

Haydn had got to know Handel's great oratorios in England, and, as we remember, he had been profoundly moved by them. Now, he was persuaded by Gottfried van Swieten, the son of Empress Maria Theresa's personal physician and director of the Court Library, and a great enthusiast for the choral music of Handel, to rewrite *The Seven Words of the Saviour on the Cross* as an oratorio. He also added a purely instrumental interlude which was scored for a large wind band and which is one of the most astonishing and sinister pieces of music Haydn ever wrote. The new work was first performed at Vienna in 1797. Its success may have inspired Haydn to begin work on *The Creation*, the libretto of which, based on Milton's *Paradise Lost*, had been given him by Salomon before he left England. On 15th December 1796, Haydn's old friend J. G. Albrechtsberger wrote to their mutual pupil Ludwig van Beethoven that Haydn had come to see Albrechtsberger the day before and was occupied with the idea of a big oratorio which he intended to call *The Creation*. Haydn improvised some of it for Albrechtsberger and the latter thought it would be very good.

Haydn spent almost the whole of 1797 and part of 1798 on the composition of *The Creation*. The sixty-five-year-old master was fully aware of the responsibilities of such a vast subject; and the endless sketches, first drafts, second drafts and last-minute changes which can be seen in various manuscripts in Viennese libraries show that never had he taken his task more seriously, nor approached the subject with more reverence.

Van Swieten had gathered together a group of aristocrats who agreed to guarantee Haydn a sum of 500 ducats and to finance and arrange the first performance, which took place under Haydn's direction at the Schwarzenberg Palace on the Neuer Markt on 29th and 30th April 1798. The success of the work was such that it had to be repeated on 7th and 10th May. Shortly afterwards, Haydn announced that he would print the score by subscription. After further revision, the first public performance took place at the Burgtheater in Vienna on 19th March 1799, with Haydn conducting and Salieri, the Emperor's *Capellmeister*, at the pianoforte. Such was the excitement among the populace that eighteen mounted guards and a dozen policemen were required to keep order. The audience was exceptionally large and the receipts amounted to 4,088 fl. 30 kr., a sum which had never been taken by any Viennese theatre. One of Haydn's biographers, Carpani, was an eye-witness: 'I was there and can assure you never to have experienced anything like it. The flower of Vienna's literary and musical world was gathered in the hall. . . . Profound silence, the most undivided attention, a—I would say—religious respect obtained from that moment when the violins made their first *coup d'archet.*'

The construction of *The Creation* is, musically speaking, traditional. That is, Haydn uses the customary division of choruses, accompanied recitatives (usually for descriptive passages), arias and *secco* recitatives (with harpsichord and lower strings only). It seems quite clear that he retained the old-fashioned Italian *secco* for reasons of colour; in these brief sections, the listener has a chance to rest from the vast sound of the choruses and the largest orchestra Haydn ever employed. The choruses contain passages for solo voices or for the soloists as a group. The orchestra itself consists of three flutes, two oboes, two clarinets, two bassoons, doublebassoon, two horns, two trumpets, three trombones, kettledrums and strings; and never is Haydn more brilliant and resourceful than in the instrumentation of *The Creation*. The boundless loneliness of the introduction, a 'description of chaos', is positively breath-taking, not only in its harmonic daring—it uses harmonic ideas which look forward to the discoveries of composers sixty and seventy years later—but also in its marvellous orchestration (the wild sweep of the clarinet, and the almost sinister, grey wood-wind scoring, which so movingly depicts the earth surrounded by swirling darkness). And when has Haydn— or, indeed, any other composer—surpassed the serene unearthly beauty of the E major introduction to Part III, describing that magical moment of early morning when the sun first touches 'the rosy clouds'? (It is here that the three flutes are used.)

There are, of course, sublime high-points: the unforgettable exaltation of 'and there was light', a tremendous, overwhelming *fortissimo* following a whispered introduction; the shining brightness of the first sunrise, and the soft sheen of the strings as Uriel the Archangel—all the narrators are archangels—describes in hushed tones the first moonlight; 'the heavens are telling', the chorus, based on Psalm XIX, 1, that ends the first part, in which we feel that truly Haydn was there when 'the morning stars sang together, and all the sons of God shouted for joy'; Raphael's awesome description of the impenetrable mystery of birth, in which divided violins, cellos and the bottom range of the double-basses (a brilliant afterthought—originally this was a *secco* recitative) underline God's command: 'Be fruitful, grow and multiply!'

The descriptions of nature, of birds and beasts, are not without their moments of humour. How the audience must have been delighted with the roars of the 'tawny lion' (with *fortissimo* double-bassoon and trombones), the snarls of the tiger, and the loathsome course of the crawling serpent (No. 21). Some of the arias are as direct and simple as folk song, but their melodies, time after time, have the beauty, strength and grace that was Haydn's greatest secret; such an aria is Uriel's 'In native worth', a joyous affirmation of the brotherhood of man. And only Haydn could have written the lovely soprano aria 'With verdure clad', a gentle, happy song to the early spring.

Perhaps only an old and very wise man could have written *The Creation*; and perhaps, too, only a man in his sixties could so poignantly recapture the bliss of the early morning, the magic of the moonlight, or the rapture of a spring day: these things which he knows will soon retreat beyond his grasp. The words which Carpani wrote on hearing a Haydn Mass one Sunday morning might well have been said of *The Creation*: 'In 1799,' he writes, 'I was confined to bed in Vienna by a fever. The bells announced a Mass at a church not far from my room: my boredom got the better of my prudence, and I rose and went to console myself with a little music. I inquired as I entered, and found it was the festival of St. Anne and that they were going to perform a Mass of Haydn's in B flat major, which I had never before heard. Scarcely had it begun before I felt myself affected. I broke out into a perspiration, my headache went away: I left the church with a cheerfulness to which I had long been a stranger, and the fever never returned.' The Mass in B flat Major is Haydn's 1796 Mass for the Princess, the *Mass of St. Bernard of Offida*, or the *Heiligmesse*.

In the midst of composing *The Creation* Haydn wrote one of his most famous pieces, the Austrian National Anthem, based on a text by Lorenz Leopold Haschka. Again Haydn worked very hard to achieve the simple and lovely melody which has become part of the world's musical heritage. Like

many famous melodies this one was subject to some curious transforma-
tions; it has now become the German National Anthem (the Austrians use,
rather inappropriately, a Freemason song which may have been, but was
probably not, composed by Mozart), and Haydn's immortal melody is even
today sung as a Protestant hymn in England and America under the title
'Glorious things of Thee are spoken.' Haydn also incorporated variations on

Haydn's manuscript of the *Emperor's Hymn*

the melody in one of his string quartets from Op. 76 (a series of six works
which were composed in 1796 and 1797). In these beautiful and famous
quartets Haydn combines his older, intimate quartet style with that of the
symphonic quartets written for Salomon in London. Indeed, they are only
surpassed by his last two finished quartets composed in 1799 and known to
us as Op. 77. The third quartet which was to go with these two remained
unfinished, and was published as a fragment some years later ('Op. 103').

The enormous success of *The Creation* must have suggested to both Haydn
and van Swieten the idea that they should create still another oratorio. Van
Swieten chose as his subject *The Seasons*, a poem by James Thomson, which
he translated and edited. Haydn composed the first part in 1799 but continued more slowly, hindered by illness for his health was breaking down
after a lifetime of hard work, on the remaining sections until 1801. The first
performance took place on 24th April 1801, and was repeated on 27th April
and 1st May. It was sponsored by a group of noblemen in the same way as
The Creation had been. The first public performance took place at the
Redoutensaal on 29th May 1801.

Thomson's poem provided Haydn with obvious effects for tone painting, but he found it difficult to put the work into a satisfying form; and it must have cost him almost superhuman effort to achieve that delicate balance between humour, sentiment and depth which characterize this extraordinary oratorio. Just as in *The Creation*, there are moments of unforgettable grandeur; Haydn uses his enormous orchestra with his customary virtuosity and in some respects *The Seasons* is like a panorama of Haydn's whole creative life. There are some parts of it that sound like a folk song, there are some parts that sound like an enormous mass, there are sections (such as the middle of summer) when we feel that Haydn is looking down at his people prostrated by the summer heat. There are times, too, when an unutterable sadness seems to pervade the music, almost as if Haydn himself knew that this celebration of the beauty of the world would be his artistic swansong. There is a hunting chorus with four horns which seems to recall those gay and carefree days at Eisenstadt when the gentry were greeted upon their return from the hunt with Haydn's 'Horn Signal' Symphony (No. 31), and to end autumn there is a vigorous drunken scene in which Haydn introduces 'Turkish instruments' in the manner of the 'Military' Symphony. That Haydn himself was conscious of this panorama-like aspect of *The Seasons* is shown in the air which the peasant sings in the first part; Haydn used the famous melody from the second movement of the 'Surprise' Symphony instead of taking van Swieten's advice and using a tune from a popular German opera; nobody knows any melody from the long-forgotten German opera, while the tune Haydn used is almost universally known and loved. Later Haydn said to his pupil Sigismund Neukomm that when he was writing 'Winter', he realized that he had become an old man and was at the end of his creative powers.

In these last years, after having composed the *Harmoniemesse* in 1802, his last major work, Haydn undertook to compose the accompaniments for a number of Scottish songs for which several publishers, foremost among them the Edinburgh firm of George Thomson, paid him a handsome fee. It is now known that Haydn engaged his pupils (among them Neukomm) to do some of this work.

Haydn was also concerned with putting his affairs in order, and in 1805 he had his faithful copyist, Johann Elssler, draw up a thematic catalogue which is the basis of our knowledge of Haydn's authentic works; this supplements the so-called *Entwurf-Katalog* which Haydn and Elssler's father began to make in about 1765. Happily, the *Entwurf-Katalog* still exists. By this time the trade in Haydn's compositions had become a major financial consideration for most music publishers and copyists, and they did not hesitate to attach Haydn's name to works by other composers; to see how serious the situation was, one only need recall that for the 107 authentic symphonies there are 150 spurious ones. Haydn's own catalogue is often incomplete and contains many omissions, duplications and inaccuracies, for he was an old man with a failing memory when he made it, but without it any attempt to establish what he actually composed would have been nearly hopeless.

Haydn's wife finally died in 1802, too late for Haydn to think of re-marrying. Luigia Polzelli had managed to extract from him a written promise that he would marry no one but her, and armed with this document she herself married and moved to Italy.

Honours poured in on the ageing composer from all over the world: medals and titles from Amsterdam, Stockholm, St. Petersburg, Paris—and there seems no end to the list of persons and institutions who wished to do homage to this great and modest composer. Every sort of traveller, musical and otherwise, came to pay respects to the comfortable house in the Untere Steingasse. Princess Maria Hermenegild saw that his old age was comfortable and even had Prince Nicolaus II give him the best Esterházy wine for his table and the Prince's own doctors and medicines for his frail and dying body.

Haydn died on 31st May 1809 of old age and exhaustion at the age of seventy-seven. In the days preceding his death his servants would carry him to the piano where he would play his Austrian anthem, *Gott erhalte Franz den Kaiser* ('God save Franz our Emperor'). The French were bombarding Vienna and when a cannon ball fell near the house, Haydn held out his arms to the terrified servants and said to them seriously: 'Don't be afraid, where Haydn is nothing can befall you.' The French then occupied Vienna and Napoleon placed a guard of honour at Haydn's door. Elssler took Haydn's death mask which still exists. The next day we have a graphic report of Haydn's burial from the diary of a friend of his, J. G. Rosenbaum: '1 June. A hot day, stifling dust. No procession. In the afternoon at five burial of the great and immortal singer of *The Creation* and *The Seasons*, Joseph Haydn. All the theatres are closed. All the marshals and generals have left. Afternoon at four o'clock with Rodler to Haydn's burial. He lay in his large room dressed in black, not at all distorted, at his feet lay the seven honorary medals from Paris, Russia, Sweden and our own *Bürger-medaille*. After five o'clock Haydn was placed in an oak casket and taken to the Gumpendorf church, carried around it three times, blessed and put in the cemetery at the Hundsturmer Linie. Not one single *Capellmeister* of Vienna accompanied his corpse.'

It was the French occupation which made the funeral so quiet, and it had a grim, rather shocking epilogue. Prince Nicolaus II was given permission to take Haydn's body and rebury it at Eisenstadt, but did not attempt to do so until 1820. When Haydn's body was exhumed, it was found to be headless. Two friends of Haydn's had removed his head—they said they wanted to protect it from 'desecration'—and agreed to return it when the Prince offered a reward for its recovery.

The Prince broke his promise and gave no reward, but so did the possessors of Haydn's skull; they sent another skull to be buried with Haydn's body. Eventually they gave the skull to the Society of the Friends of Music, and in 1954 it was finally united with the rest of the body in the grave under the Bergkirche in Eisenstadt where so much of his beautiful music had been given to the world.

Suggestions for Further Reading

Every history of music pays considerable attention to Haydn and his works. Among the numerous biographies dealing with his career, character and music, the following seem to be specially worthy of attention:

The Collected Correspondence and London Notebooks of Joseph Haydn, edited by H. C. Robbins Landon (Barrie and Jenkins, 1959)
Haydn: a Creative Life in Music, by Karl Geiringer (Allen and Unwin, 1947)
Haydn, by Rosemary Hughes (Dent, 1962. *Master Musicians* series)
Haydn Symphonies, by H. C. Robbins Landon (B.B.C. Publications, 1966)
Joseph Haydn: his Life in Contemporary Pictures, by László Somfai, translated by Mari Kuttner and Karoly Ravasz. (Faber and Faber, 1969)

The above book contains in its commentary much of the early biographies of the composer written by Georg August Griesinger and Christoph Dies, both of whom obtained their information from Haydn himself. A short introductory book is *Joseph Haydn: his life and work*, by Henry Raynor (Boosey and Hawkes, 1961, *The Great Masters* series).

A Summary of Haydn's Works

Operas

Seventeen operas for the theatre and five for a puppet theatre. Seven of these have been completely or almost completely lost. They include the comic operas:

Lo speziale (The Apothecary) 1768
L'infedeltà delusa (Inconstancy deluded), 1773
Il mondo della luna (The world on the moon), 1777

and the serious operas:

L'isola disabitata (The desert island), 1779
Armida, 1784

Oratorios

The Creation, 1798
The Seasons, 1801

Church Music

Mass of St. Bernard of Offida, 1796

Many miscellaneous works and fourteen Masses; these include:

Missa in Tempore Belli, or *Paukenmesse* (Mass in time of War, or Drum-roll Mass), 1796–7
Nelson Mass, or *Missa in Angustiis*, 1798
Schöpfungsmesse (Creation Mass), 1801
Harmoniemesse (Wind-band Mass), 1802

Symphonies

About 107 works, all except one of which have survived; they include:

A Summary of Haydn's Works

Nos. 82 to 87, The 'Paris Symphonies', 1785–87
No. 92, The 'Oxford Symphony', 1789
Nos. 93–104, The 'London' or 'Salomon Symphonies', 1791–95

Concertos

Thirty-seven concertos for organ, piano, violin, cello, double-bass and horn and
   Trumpet Concerto, 1796

Chamber Music

   62 string quartets
   45 piano trios
   and many works for other small groups of instruments

Piano

   62 sonatas
   and many small pieces for piano

Songs

More than 60 solo songs, among which are two sets of 6 Canzonets (with English words), 1794–95.
   Haydn, sometimes with the help of friends and students, arranged accompaniments for violin, cello and piano to nearly 400 Scottish, Welsh and Irish folk songs after he had become known in England.

Index

Index

Index

479